THE MOUNT MORIAH
STUDIES

By

HARALD WYNDHAM

THE MOUNT MORIAH STUDIES, by Harald Wyndham, is published by
Blue Scarab Press in Pocatello, Idaho in April, 1989.
Photographs were taken by the author.

ISBN Number: 0-937179-03-5

Special thanks to Dr. Robert Anderson and Dr. James Aho
for reviewing the manuscript.

This book was printed for Blue Scarab Press by
LITHO PRINTING of Pocatello, Idaho.

The occasional use of explicit language may be offensive
to some readers.

Address all correspondence to Blue Scarab Press
243 S. 8th Street Pocatello, Idaho 83201

This book is dedicated to

STEPHEN W. HAWKING
Mathematician and Physicist

His courage and creativity
showcase the human spirit.
Scarce able to move,
he travels the cosmos.

ALL THINGS in nature work silently. They come into Being and
possess nothing. They fulfill their function and make no claim.
All things alike do their work, and then we see them subside.
When they have reached their bloom, each returns to its origin.
Returning to their origin means rest, or fulfillment of destiny.
This reversion is the eternal law. To know that law is wisdom.

                         -- Lao Tzu, Tao Te Ching

I have seen the business that God has given to the sons of men
to be busy with. He has made everything beautiful in its time;
also he has put eternity into man's mind, yet so that he cannot
find out what God has done from the beginning to the end. I know
that there is nothing better for them than to be happy and enjoy
themselves as long as they live; also that it is God's gift to
man that every one should eat and drink and take pleasure in all
his toil. I know that whatever God does endures forever; nothing
can be added to it, nor anything taken from it; God has made it
so, in order that men should fear before Him. That which is,
already has been; that which is to be, already has been; and
God seeks what has been driven away.

                         -- Ecclesiastes 3: 10-15

We regard all created beings as sacred and important, for
everything has a *wochangi,* or influence, which can be given
to us, through which we may gain a little more understanding
if we are attentive. We should understand well that all things
are the works of the Great Spirit. We should know that He is
within all things: the trees, the grasses, the rivers, the
mountains and all the four-legged animals, and the winged
peoples; and even more important, we should understand that
He is also above all these things and peoples.

                         -- Black Elk, Lakota Sioux

For He knows we are but dust, and that our days are few and
brief, like grass, like flowers, blown by the wind and gone forever.

                         -- Psalm 103: 14-16

I celebrate myself and sing myself,
and what I assume you shall assume,
for every atom belonging to me as good belongs to you.

-- Walt Whitman, SONG OF MYSELF

What thou lovest well is thy true heritage--
What thou lovest well shall not be reft from thee.

The ant's a centaur in his dragon world.
Pull down thy vanity, it is not man
Made courage, or made order, or made grace,
    Pull down thy vanity, I say pull down.
Learn of the green world what can be thy place
In scaled invention or true artistry.
Pull down thy vanity,
                    Paquin pull down!
The green casque has outdone your elegance.

-- Ezra Pound, CANTO LXXXI

And the end of all our exploring
will be to arrive where we started
and know the place for the first time.

-- T.S. Eliot, LITTLE GIDDING

Those not busy being born
are busy dying.

-- Bob Dylan

TO THE READER

Dear friend, this year of words
attempts to express some guesses
and grapplings toward understanding
that go back to the beginning for me.

The setting is local in one sense,
but cosmic in another. Not so much
place as space and time, nor my life
so much as the life I am part of,
which includes your life also.

The form is a puzzle and a metaphor,
implying more than it reveals.
It is twelve strands twisted
twelve times. It is carefully
structured and shamelessly
spontaneous, risking everything.

Does it succeed? Only you can know.
For myself, it is complete after
thirteen years and ready to have
a life of its own in the world.
I have given it all I can.
Now it is up to you.

Pocatello, Idaho
Nov. 11, 1988

1.

Alpha begins it
if there is Beginning, black buds in the cottonwoods,
skeletal branches, grass uncombed of last summer's leaves /
ADENINE the four-bound gospel, phosphate-to-sugar containing
all options / APRIL AND ARIES, ASTRONOMY, ALCHEMY /
myself unfolding as well, energy in bloodcell,
boisterous, pleased to be alive,
hands raised overhead to the trees /
BEGINS WITH A BANG!
(HUBBLE/HAWKING)
10^{-43} SECOND PLANCK TIME
BEFORE WHICH ALL WE CAN CALL IT IS
GOD/GOTT/GUT (GRAND UNIFIED THEORY) THE ALPHA
EXPANDING/COOLING AT 10^{-35} SEC STRONG & WEAK FORCES

BREAK APART/DISSIPATE/PRECIPITATE AT 10^{28^0} KELVIN OUTRUSHING /
firstborn of Olympia, Pella, son of Achilles, he conquered the world /
time for explorations and armies, birdsong
above traffic, the plastic carapaces of fast food
blown against wrought-iron fences /
Optic chiasma, fusion
of visions poured
through a vitreous humor,
talented pupil / *who routed the Persians*
at Arbela, 331, the phalanx piercing the core shouting
kill Darius! kill Darius! scattering armies / MATTER/ANTIMATTER
DESTROYING THEMSELVES AT 10^{-32} SEC LEAVING A RESIDUE/DUST/FROM WHICH BEGAN
STARS/MAN/ALLTHINGS LIGHT&DARK / a deathmask penetrated
by grassblades in this month / *Bucephalus the*
untameable tamed to ride him to India /
fovea centralis, sclera
enchanted iris the shutter opening
bright   worlds bent refracted myopic and beautiful /
the grain in the stone, carved to a lotus, human pattern overlaying
nature, cut in a circle, characters also, the pathway visible
in a stand of weeds, curving twist of the cottonwood,
scattering of stones, a place
for everyone / QUARKS OF SIX
FLAVORS, THREE COLORS
BINDING THE PIECES (AT 10^{-6} SEC)
ELECTRONS STILL FREE IN THE BLACKNESS /
or Marco Polo following cameltracks into China /
Things change always, the big trees cut down
leaving a hole in the sky, grain of soil curved beneath grass,
and god is too enormous to be named, flux dominates, people
die, those that we love, my mother and father
>   in this month of cancer, leukemia /
10^5 YEARS INTO IT, 3000^0 K,
THE FIRST ATOMS
THEN QUASARS BURSTING WITH LIGHT /

                    died of excesses, of drink and of women,
               beloved of troops, carted back in a solid gold coffin
          at age thirty-two / when it snows I stand under the fir tree,
     as under the skirts of an oracle, bodiless, deathless, thinking about
          MARY ELIZABETH FINGERLOS, 1926, part of the process,
               comprehending nothing.

                              2.

                    Snowfall is magical--Chinese!--
                         white on black calligraphy:
                                   treelimbs drawn in space,
                         crisp bootprints, textures
               of snowfilled bark, waterfall whiteness
          filling the infinite distance between trees, filling
     the mind with deadening sound, imposing silence /
CYTOSINE linkage / cochlea shaped like a snail, perilymph fluid
          vibrating hairs of precise length /
                    and by noon of the third day it has all melted off
                    leaving the paths muddy for walking /
                         JOSEPH NUSSBAUMER, 1923, BORN
                                   IN OBERAGEN, SCHWEIZ /
                    and the family drives out
               to visit the place one week later and finds
          the heap of flowers withered, brown already, covered
     with snow. In this way, the dead depart on journeys, returning
to visit perhaps in dreams, suddenly present, and we are overwhelmed /
          OVERHEAD THE RAM, SCARCE VISIBLE, WITH UNNAMED MEMBERS
               NUMBERED, CATALOGUED, A PATTERN FOR WATCHERS
                    BEFORE INCANDESCENCE / malleus to
                         incus, stapes with oval window
                              and the three canals
                         for balancing, cleverly crafted
                    repetition, selection, combination /
               but for the most part, we are alone with our feelings,
          old flowers thrown onto the sexton's truckbed, new violets

                              11

opening beneath creamy skies behind stirred branches clotted with buds
                as if the long-awaited bride stepped off the last dark sleeper
                        in a gauze gown embroidered with/scented with violets
                                and her bachelor in bluejeans,
                                        mud on his boots, takes her hand
                                                and the dance begins /
                                THE RED WARRIOR WITH TWO
                        DOGS, DEIMOS AND PHOBOS, RUNNING
                THROUGH OUR SKY THIS DAY OF HIS DOUBLEYEAR
        BRINGING TRANSFORMING FIRE, MAGIC, INTO THE MELTINGPOT /
accompanied by pilgrims of all nationalities, Basques, Greeks,
        Italians, Swedes, Spaniards, Japanese and the Irish nuns,
                wedding guests, twilight behind black trees,
                        night cry of homecoming birds /
                                metal to leather riveted, harness,
                                        stirrup, shield strap,
                                lightweight battlesword and spear
                        of the long shaft for stabbing in phalanx,
                the helmet crafted to protect all but the fierce eyes /
        PHLOGISTON/NAPALM/HIROSHIMA/CRUCIBLE/VULCAN /
collecting twigsnap windthrill breathsong the textured air alive /
        flute soft, if you listen, if you watch, attentive,
                crimson cloud, thinnest crescent moon, the
                        irresitable, dancing
                                girl.

                                3.

                                Claudius Ptolemaeus c. 130 a.d.
                                        extended Hipparchus into
                                full predictive epicycles that lasted
                        till Copernicus (1.5 millenia) not bad,
                though we know now that it's rubbish /
        frontal, temporal, occipital, parietal superba,
where lies speech, touch, vision, memory and thought--
                none of it true in the everlasting sense, a viewpoint

                                12

sealed in cerebellum, in blood-rushing darkness,
enlightened by chemical fire, sparks
gapping the synapse /
We have landed men
on the moon, Galileo, that you
mapped in amazement naming oceans/seas
that are more tranquil than even you believed, being
airless waste, residue of dust, frigid. We have explored
the bottoms of the sea and can circumnavigate (Magellan) the globe in hours,
describe atomic particles, peer into every corner--
nothing is forbidden us--there are no
mysteries, although for such knowledge
even the tiniest grain of life
remains a mystery,
none of our questions answered
about who we are, why we are here /
5000 years ago, Egypt, the year divided into 365 days,
Aristarchus discovered the wobbling axis, Eratosthenes
that the world is round (230 B.C.) collecting observations
from ten thousand years of stargazing,
Stonehenge, the starwheel in Wyoming,
when to plant, when to make war /
corpus callosum, hypothalamus
diencephalon /
THE WRIGHT BROS AT KITTY HAWK,
FORD UP IN MICHIGAN, MACHINING METALS
LIKE HEPHAESTUS AT HIS FORGE, WIRE/CABLE AND
GOD KNOWS HOW MANY COMPOUNDS THAT NEVER EXISTED BEFORE /
GUANINE creative energy / MILO T. WOODBURY BORN 1882 / walking
under trees in new leaf, nothing significantly new since mankind
had the first clear thought--the continents adrift
so slow you can't feel it, the Dipper
points to Polaris always,
starlight older
than life on the planet /

13

The Starry Messenger, stilled for a time,
then On the Revolution of the Heavenly Spheres
putting to bed at last all that Aristotelian theocracy
so that Newton could splice light, deduce force, engorge his egocentrism /
AND MT. PALOMAR OBSERVATORY, TELESCOPES IN SATELLITES,
GOLD-VISORED GODS TETHERED TO CAPSULES ABOVE EARTH
(DEUS EX MACHINA) RATHER, THE MACHINE
HAS BECOME OUR GOD
FOR A BRIEF PERIOD /
Cold rain washes the stones
and the old man in the green '59 Pontiac
has come to bring flowers to his wife. Stands
a long time looking down at her name, then places a
small glass jar of hyacinths beside it / GAVE US ALSO DACHAU
AND THE MASS GRAVES, THIS MACHINED GOD BUILT TO LAST,
MUSTARD GAS, ACID RAIN, GREENHOUSE EFFECT AND THE SEAS
POISONED, THOUGH TO BE FAIR ALSO MUCH
MEDICINE, HEALING, LONGER LIFE
AND TELEVISION /
When the hunter rises
it is time to drive deer up the canyon
or buffalo over the cliff-face / PLASTIC GARBAGE
BLOWN AGAINST WROUGHT IRON FENCE / The white cat
has killed another sparrow. As I prepare dinner,
a host of sparrows surrounds the bird feeder.
How courageous and commonplace life is.
One goes--another takes her place.

4.

GREAT LORD OF LIGHT, GREAT LORD
OF DARKNESS, RULER
OF INFINITE, UNKNOWN REGIONS,
I RAISE MY HANDS TO YOU, MY VOICE, I BURN
THE BRAZIER, CHANT IN THE PERFUMED SMOKE, O HEAR ME /

Recorder and drum, rain washing the bushes,
filling the mind with infinitesimal music, cleaning the blind buds,
rain on the cottonwoods that twist up into the clouds,
on lilacs in new leaf, the world in its greeness,
and upturned trumpets of buttery forsythia,
rain on grandfather stones and
new aluminum markers,
on small roads and fresh grass,
raising fragrance of root-bound soil,
stems unfolding with possibilities driven by moisture,
passage of bright liquid in phloem/zylem/cambrium, rain on
the wrought iron crosses of *SISTERS MARY RAPHAEL ROHRER, MARY CLEMENT O'CONNELL,*
bathing every one of a billion cells within me also,
the peony shoots wet/crenelated, poking scarlet hoods
through black soil / soil of bones,
80 million years of ancestors,
the short, not-yet-human
oreopithecus walking upright in
primordial wonder, first touch of grief that
leads to ritual, sprinkle of leaves over corpse, worship
of powers without understanding, the earth mulched with our bodies,
THYMINE   our mythical patterning, fears and rituals begin here /
OH HEAR ME YOU POWERS THAT TRANSFORM, LORD OF THE RAM'S SKULL,
LORD OF THE CURVED HORN, OF THE POLISHED STONE,
SHAKEN SHAMAN DANCES, BAG OF TRICKS,
I CALL OUT OF DARKNESS AND SMOKE
USING THE NAME
THAT IS SECRET, UNNAMEABLE ONE
GIVE ME FERTILITY/BRING ME A SON/HEAL MY CANCER /
Who first set foot on new land, open, unspoiled /
excites the olfactory bulb, trigeminal nerve,
messengers carried in air, lilac, violets touching the mitral,
into the limbic system /   20 BILLION LIGHT YEARS AGO AND
STILL RUSHING OUTWARD THAT WALL OF HOT HYDROGEN /
At home in the luminous garden this morning,

where the poor and wealthy lie,
LEOLA MARIA DALPINO
in this section at 22 years,
treelimbs catch sunlight and sparkle,
white and lavender violets, o child come too soon /
ANCIENT, ARABIC ORDER OF NOBLES OF THE MYSTIC SHRINE, DAUGHTERS
OF THE NILE, GOD THE GRAND ARCHITECT, 33RD DEGREE MASTER (MT. MORIAH'S SILVER
GATE BEARING MASONIC EMBLEM, COMPASS AND TROWEL)
HOMEOPATHIC/HOLISTIC THERE'S-ONE-BORN-EVERY-MINUTE
ALCHEMY/THE POWER OF WORDS/POETRY
OR PARACELSUS BURNS AVICENNA 1527--
MAGIC IS METAPHORIC--
NOSTRADAMUS/HOUDINI/AUROLEUS
THEOPHRASTUS BOMBASTUS VON HOHENHEIM,
SOVERIGN GRAND INSPECTOR GENERAL ORACLE/MAGUS/KABALLA
BISON IN DARKNESS AT ALTAMIRA RITE OF PASSAGE ON CAVEWALL--
O LORD OF THE HUNT, O KALI, O GREAT ONE, FAVOR US / *MOTHER FORTUNATA, 1940*
pray for me, dark hair, luminous black eyes, times and events,
full of sorrows, pray for me *MOTHER OF FORTUNES*
virgin and child spreading arms in blessing,
I give the sign and kneel here,
do not deserve blessing,
protect me on my journeys,
O MOTHER FORTUNATA pray for me.

5.

REGULUS OVERHEAD, THE GREAT BEAR, SUNRISE
AT FIVE A.M. 107 DAYS INTO YEAR, HITLER BORN 1889
AND DACHAU LIBERATED 1945 AND NAPOLEON TO ELBA 1814, CONSTANTINOPLE
SACKED BY CRUSADERS 1204, TIME TO PLANT SWEET PEAS /
I am mad with textures--bark of the cottonwood,
gravestone grain, rough underside of leaves,
polished obsidian / papilla
tongue-touching
lips and larynx, pharnyx

                    epiglottis like a punching bag,
              specialized epiderms/channels/eustachian sensor
        how the world comes in / enormous clouds I have forgotten
   how slowly an hour passes when you lie on the warm grass observing
         seeds in the air, tiny bits streaming in spirals,
                the dead lie looking at this forever / MT MORIAH IS
                    THE BITTERNESS OF THE LORD, WHERE SOLOMON
                        BUILT THE TEMPLE AND ABRAHAM
                            BOUND ISAAC TO ALTAR /
                    composed of phosphate and sugar
              the four bases binding it / CRYPTOZOIC
            NOTHING BUT BLUE-GREEN ALGAE IN OCEANS UP TO 600
         MILLION YEARS B.C. THE PATTERN HIDDEN BEYOND FOSSILS / after dark
   GUANINE I return to lie in the cool grass, half-blue twilight, evening
         like any other in history, clouds pass like
              tremendous, leisurely beings above treebranches,
                    even the depth of sky patterned and alive /
                        TIME FOR REVOLUTIONS,
                            TAURUS IN POSITION,
                        POKE STICK IN EARTH, PENETRATE
                    WHILE ALDEBARAN DANCES ABOVE US,
              FIFTY LIGHT YEARS DISTANT, ALL THINGS CONNECTED
        AND CENTERING HERE AS WELL AS ANYWHERE, ARMIES INVADE
   AND TULIPS COME INTO BLOOM, FULL GREENING AND FLOWERING NOW,
         PLANT LETTUCE, SPINACH, WAIT FOR TOMATOES HOWEVER /
              Because we are ancient, formed at the beginning
                    from stardust as all stars were formed,
                        there is only transformation,
                            complete belonging
                    to process/nameless/unknowable
              save through metaphor/poetry/artwork of all
         manners, observing, making, receiving through senses,
   transforming in braincell workshop darkness of memory
allthings seen and unseen, possible and yet to come, patterned once only /
         First particle precipitated (string theory) exists with 2 spin

but no mass / *CLARENCE DOOLITTLE, WOODSMAN OF THE*
WORLD, 1935 / it travels between
particles carrying the force
of gravity.

6.

Ah, Walter (born this month,
1819) when I began these meditations,
my thought was to follow you--and why not?--
I, too, contain multitudes, am roughmannered, forthright,
no stander on ceremony, comrade of rich and poor, men and women the same.
Like you I saunter along in my old jeans, crumpled hat and
uncombed beard, common as a gravedigger . . . /
The voice a vibrating string,
pharynx, larynx, trachea
greek poetry /
except I have not your
optimism, your faith in democracy
and all that scientific technocracy that exploded
into wires cutting the sky, radio/video waves penetrating
our bodies with 300 channels of frenetic news about nothing. Rather,
the bomb hangs over my head. My generation more than any other
accepted your challenge to stand naked, sexually free.
We are desperate for relationship,
damaged by infidelity, having
misunderstood it all,
we seek to become famous
because we have no security in one another /
THE SEAS A SOUP OF LIFE, ARTHROPODS, MOLLUSKS
AND TRILOBITES IN THEIR GLORY FOR 300 MILLION YEARS OF ABSOLUTE
PEACE ON EARTH, LAND MASSES SMALL AND FLAT, ROCKS SPORTING LICHENS ONLY,
THINK OF THE CAMBRIAN SILENCE, GOLDEN SKIES, SHALLOW SEA /
sternocleidomastoideus that moves the head /
poetry your answer to slaughter and war,
hatred uncontrollable,

                                        the wounded farmboys,
                            dying in the hospital, all of it
                    too overwhelming, too monstrous, torn limbs
                and burst bellies, fever, gangrene choking the nostrils,
            nothing to staunch it but letters to parents, tears, a touch
and later, the poetry coming forth like a river to wash and include them all--
            what would you do with Auschwitz and Dachau, Walter,
                    that's what I need to know /
                            POET ANN HARRIS MOYES what honor,
                                to have earned that title in stone,
                                    (your daughter, my sister)
                                encourage me each time I pass /
                    hypothyroidism in children,
                a tragedy of the mind, cricoid cartilage
            and the Isthmus of Tyroid / all creatures anonymous
CYTOSINE as grass, yet present, the unnumbered birds and insects
            contributing skeleta, mulch for the soil, good manure
                    to quote you directly, none of them concerned
                        to be nameless, without history,
                            find purpose in protecting
                                the next generation /
                            TRILOBITES TEN BILLION STRONG /
                old comarado, in spite of it all
            I want to send a barbaric yawp over the rooftops,
        confound the experts and delight the desperate.
Wait down the road for me and I'll give it my best shot.

                                    7.

            Sprung from birdsong/screeches/uulations of humpbacks
                    this purest communication of personal/tribal being
                        monophonic, chanting the melody line
                                in formal pattern improvised
                                    spontaneously, singing
                                began before iceages, harmony of
                            spheres, universe alive and singing forever)
            Pythagoras, Pope Gregory, polyphony emerging (Italy)

                                    19

                  in the twelfth century/orchids/madrigals/Palestrina /
ADENINE   *collected willowbark for the salicin relieving pain when chewed*
          and trephining the skull earliest case discovered 8000 B.C.
                  Imhotep Father of Physicians (how many discoveries
                        started in Egypt, cadaver soaked in soda
                              after entrails removed,
                                    packed with resin
                        from Commiphora tree,
                  painted with frankinsence, wrapped
            for the ages, the priests chanting slogans from
      THE BOOK OF THE DEAD) *and Chinese manipulating Yin/Yang*
with needles mapping the body / first buds broken in swirls of dirt,
      air of freshcut watermelon, rainrich, sparkling beads on
            the white stones, blackstreaked names,
                        WILLIAM WILLIAMS PVT 13TH INF 8 DIV IDAHO
                              veteran of the wars, lotus
                                    wheel and stars /
                        KARL MARX/THE MASSES STRUGGLING
                  UNDER WHEELS OF LOCOMOTIVE/MECHANIZED
            IRON SHIPS/IMPROVED CANNON/REAPER AND COMBINE
      AND THE COTTON GIN/BRICK BARRACKS FOR THE WORKERS/COMPANY STORE
AND PERVASIVE SMOKESTACK STARTING THE ACID RAINS OF THIS CENTURY/AND BY
      1848 EUROPE IN FLAMES/REVOLUTION AGAINST KINGS AGAINST CAPITALISTS
            AND AFTER THE ROMANTICS TOLD US THE TRUTH ABOUT SCIENCE
                  WE BLEW THEM AWAY IN THE CIVIL WAR, FREEING
                        NO SLAVES WHEN YOU THINK ABOUT
                              TECHNOLOGY / the old
                        couple in their Sunday clothes
                  fill a coffee can at the dripping spigot /
            Emmer began it, after the last ice age, crossed
      with goat grass to become dependent on human distribution,
Jacob vs Esau, poked stick and plow, domesticating cattle, Jericho inhabited
      long before Biblical times, ritual of seasons, starmaps, and
            the priests leading them into the fields singing /
                  My grandmother's face comes to me now

                                    20

as if this were the curved lane
to Bayrischzell, although
I should be home spading the garden,
transforming the dead sparrow into fertilizer,
instead of walking here, the western sky dark copper
against blue rose, cottonwoods with half-opened buds, her face
painted between them like the moon, delicate, white, connection in the
mind only, metaphoric salvation, artwork of the soul /
LAST STAND OF CRAZYHORSE NOT CUSTER THAT SUMMER OF 1876
WHIPPING CROOK AT THE ROSEBUD AND THEN
THE LITTLE BIG HORN, BETRAYED
BY HIS OWN, JAILED
AND MURDERED (FT ROBINSON 1877)
THE STRANGE ONE SAW THE END IN THE CLOUDS
BUT WOULD NOT EMBRACE LOCOMOTIVE/RESERVATION /
then around 1700's the Germans began injecting formaldehyde,
mercuric chloride, zinc chloride, alcohol into the veins to prevent
mortification of war dead being shipped home for burial,
from which we have the painted face in the box and
all that artificial expensive folderol
right down to the little rollers
two-ton cement vault
and the great American tradition
of funerals, as the sonofabitch told me
when we had mother cremated / whole families strolling,
beefy, belligerent mammas/pappas with kids running everywhere,
widows cruising in simonized caddies, juveniles with radios blasting,
balding professors glide by on their ten-speeds and
blue-jeaned lovers saunter among the stones, surely
those buried beneath us are reincarnated here,
who knew the color of the sky in 1922
lived through two world wars
never imagined television, voiceless
while we walk and talk in the urgency of
our times, which are already faded newspapers lining a
dresser drawer / Hippocrates 400 B.C. to Galen's experiments

21

from which Avicenna, The Canon Of Medicine and Vesalius' anatomy
onward and upward, the silver caduceus on the mercedes benz /
by the time of Vivaldi and Bach it was peaking,
strings counterbalanced, well-tempered clavier
all of it worked out mathematically
except the deep voice
born of the muse, from which "music"
and Beethoven stomping through orchestras,
pushing the singers beyond capability, no longer
province of the man in the street, but Vienna Boys Choir,
voices specialized as instruments/machinery/technology castrating the spirit
although god knows we love to listen to it on a compact disc
not realizing what we have lost / my soul
slips into the drift and flux,
pupils expand to the darkness,
the space above me
widens as trees reach upward,
extending into cool air where birds
navigate between branches and I am lost out of my body,
absorbed into sandgrains, subatomic structures, infinite
distances between leaves on the tree, at the edge of sleep or dying,
whirling in the nameless places, what
does it signify?

8.

ASCENSION DAY, ALDEBARAN THE EYE
AND PLEIADES THE SHOULDER,
CRAB NEBULA, ZEUS
IN LOVE WITH EUROPA, FOLLOW
THE ARC FROM THE DIPPER TO ARCTURUS,
THE WRIGHT BROS PATENTING THE AIRPLANE AND
FARMER KILLED BY HAIL IN LUBBOCK, TEXAS 1930, SMALL
NOTATIONS ON THE ROCK OF AGES / fourteen million years old, lower jaw
found by Lewis in India, upper by Leakey in Africa, Miocene
Period, earliest direct ancestor, Ramapithecus /

The dead have their Mardis Gras /
                force that arises between particles
                            of electric charge,
                quantum of energy, a photon with
        no mass, spin of 1, exchanging the force
    or emitted as visible light, Max Planck 1900 /
    see how they embalm the grounds with flowers, roads so crowded
with buicks and pontiacs it's dangerous to be here, once-a-year party,
    although we don't bring lunch out to eat with our ancestors,
                there is the ritual clipping of grass around stones /
            EARTH THE ELEMENT, VENUS DOMINANT
                    TWO DAY YEAR AND FOUR MONTH DAY
                        WITH TEMPERATURES
            460° C AT THE SURFACE
        AND SULFURIC ACID RAIN, SO MUCH FOR
    YOUR GODDESS OF LOVE, PROBED BY THE SOVIETS /
    Heisenberg put it off-balance, nature always one step ahead--
the more you look at it, the less you know where it is--
    so put that in your pipe and smoke it, Albert . . . /
        Exiles, all of them--*ARRISTIZABAL, OMAEHAVERREA,*
        KAMAMURA and dark spanish rose
                    JULIA ESPOSA DE EDUARDO ARRIZABALAGA,
                        age 21 coming here,
                    a traveller passing through
                from one combination to the next /
            WRITE IT ALL DOWN IF YOU CARE TO. PENTECOST
        IS CELEBRATED, HARVEST OF THE FIRST FRUITS, JOHN
BROWN BORN IN 1800 AND THE LUSITANIA TORPEDOED 1915,
        WRITE IT ALL DOWN, THEN WHAT? THE CRAB
            CONTINUES TO EXPAND IN THE BELT OF ORION /
            all pressure to succeed receeds,
                    light passed through bone china
                        suffuses my brain /
                take a scrap of bone and teeth,
        extrapolate what he ate for lunch /

23

                    how the heart survives,
                        sealed like a honeycomb,
                                our lives mean everything and nothing
                                        pebbles by the roadside
                            grains of the galaxies,
                    we, too, contain universes /
            Hypothesizing that all of it came from compacted light
        the first word of God which even in this century sticks
THYMINE like a cockleburr on the sleeve of nuclear physics /
            then fight the academy for twenty years trying to prove it,
                just one more monkey trial, uncertainty
                        about origins and the makeup of atoms and stars.

                            9.

                                TOOK OSIRIS IN PIECES SHE
                                    GATHERED FROM EARTH'S END
                                AND PRAYED TO RE, THE SUN GOD,
                        PRAYED FOR HIS WHOLENESS TO BE RESTORED
                    LIKE SCARAB FROM MANUREPILE, LIFE OUT OF NOTHINGNESS,
            AND THE PRIESTS OF ISIS PROCESSING INTO THE TEMPLE, CHANTING IT /
CYTOSINE Because new life flames in the trees, lilac/forsythia, sunbursts
        of color enveloping air with fragrance at sunset,
                rising from pavement wet with night rains in morning,
                    memories carried by rainsmells, faces
                    we love, winking at us
                                from edges of thought /
                        QUASI-STELLAR OBJECTS AT THE OUTER
                    EDGE OF THE UNIVERSE (20,000,000,000 LIGHT YRS
                DISTANT EXPANDING STILL AT 90% LIGHTSPEED) BLACK HOLES
        IN THE CENTER DRIVING OUT MORE ENERGY THAN A TRILLION SUNS,
    THESE FOUNTAINS OF RAW LIGHT SEEN AS XRAYS / *DROWNED THE ROMANTICS,*
        DROWNED SHELLEY OFF PISA, WASHED UP LIKE A MACKEREL, TRELAWNEY
                SNATCHING HIS HEART FROM THE ASHES, DROWNED BYRON
                    IN SORROWS IN HIS OWN FLUIDS, BLED LIFELESS,
                        AND BEETHOVEN DISGUSTED, TEARING
                            THE 3RD SYMPHONY COVERSHEET

AND TO HELL WITH NAPOLEON /

A day for remembering all who have died

in battle, in life struggles and not only soldiers

though enough of them, truly, after two world wars, Korea, Vietnam

not to mention the Great Rebellion (scarce thought of in Idaho), the Mayor

and American Legion Commander make speeches, the old boys

fire a blank salute into the treetops

while a few veterans not yet ready for speeches

stand in the shade, to one side,

remembering Khe Sanh /

MAY YOUR KA AND YOUR BA LIVE EVER,

MAY HORUS GREET YOU IN THE GOLDEN LAND,

OH HATHOR, GODDESS OF AFTERLIFE, OSIRIS THE JUDGE,

THIS SOUL COMES ON A LONG JOURNEY UP THE NILE OF YEARS, TEFNUT

GODDESS OF MOISTURE, GEB UNDERFOOT AND NUT OVERHEAD,   RECEIVE THIS SOUL /

I am here also, in my old pants, sandals, faded shirt and cap,

who have none of my family here, though all are mine,

bringing sprigs of lilac in both hands

to lay on the grave of UNKNOWN MAN

buried by the county 1950

as if at Arlington with an honor guard,

stopping by *DAVID CANDLAND'S* handmade stone

and by so many infants and migrants, remembering heroes,

the unmarked graves of life-warriors the world over, none of them

wasted or without purpose (though we cannot know what purpose) who sacrificed

everything, even their names, all of them children born beautiful,

taking their chances, broken to pieces, scattered /

AND SEVENTY-THOUSAND DIED IN THIS FIELD,

ANOTHER HUNDRED THOUSAND OVER THERE,

WATERLOO, JUNE, 1815

BLUCHER ROUTED AND WELLINGTON'S BOYS

HANGING ON IN THE THICK OF IT TILL NEY CRUMBLED

AND THE PRUSSIANS HELD ON AND NAPOLEON HIMSELF COULDN'T

KEEP IT TOGETHER, MARCHED OFF IN THE RAIN, ON FOOT, MID TROOPS,

A VICTORY OF CANNON AND TIMING, BLOOD MIXED WITH FIELDGRASS / Tell me,

what does it matter, after the battle and burial, what
you believed in, whether you fought or resisted,
whether you chose God or denied everything--
the wind touches the inside branches
heavy with earthsmell,
and night comes on like a living
creature, blowing out candles inside us,
and there are no gods in the darkness / AND
BYRON: I FIND IT EQUALLY DIFFICULT TO KNOW WHAT TO BELIEVE
IN THIS WORLD AND WHAT NOT TO BELIEVE. AND BEETHOVEN (MISSA SOLEMNIS AND THE
NINTH NOTWITHSTANDING, DEAFNESS, KARL'S REBELLION, MANKIND ALWAYS
A DISAPPOINTMENT): GOD ABOVE ALL--GOD HAS NEVER
DESERTED ME. 30,000 MOURNERS,1827 /
No inch of soil but contains
names and voices,
memories, particles, traces.
What will you know of me in two thousand years?
No more than I know of you today.
Everything and nothing. All that we are. /
REMEMBER FRIENDS, AS YOU PASS BY, AS YOU ARE NOW, SO ONCE WAS I,
AS I AM NOW, SO YOU WILL BE, PREPARE FOR DEATH AND FOLLOW ME /
Walter born the 31st of this month 1816. /
HOLY ISIS, MOTHER OF ALL, PRAY FOR US
SCATTERED IN FRAGMENTS, UNGATHERED.

10.

AND THE SUN ITSELF
TAKES 230 MILLION YEARS
TO CIRCUMNAVIGATE THE GALAXY AT 220KM/SEC
IN THE ARM OF ORION, THE MILKY WAY SPREADING OUT
ONE HUNDRED THOUSAND LIGHT YEARS ACROSS AND (JESUS!) IT'S
ONLY ONE IN THE LOCAL CLUSTER OF TWENTY OR SO INCLUDING ANDROMEDA
TWO HUNDRED MILLION STARS STRETCHED DOWN THE SUMMER NIGHT SKY /
the unexpected rain beats the cottonwoods
lifting rank, bitter odor into the air /

26

                    emergence of mollusks/cephalopods
                            and the first chordates,
                    clams, starfish, corals, decline
              of trilobites over 75 M years and volcanic
         mountains from Newfoundland to Alabama boiling the soup /
        come in my old shoes, clopping the lanes, glass of white wine
in one hand, torn bread in the other, to be savored beneath black limbs /
        TYCHO'S FALSE NOSE OF GOLD AND SILVER NOT PART OF THE BARGAIN,
            HE (KEPLER) INHERITED ALL ELSE, MEASUREMENTS NOT
              HERETICAL IN THEMSELVES (BEING NUMBERS)
                    BUT DRIVING COFFIN NAILS INTO PTOLEMY
                        # 1) THE ORBITS ARE
                    ELIPTICAL, NOT PERFECT CIRCLES
              AS IF GOD ABHORRS WHAT IS NOT ECCENTRIC /
         interwoven textures of leaves in liquid space overhead,
        tiny winged seeds twirling to float by surface tension on water
GUANINE before sinking to join the others, wife and children gone
        and what is genuinely myself rising up like a belldiver
            to breathe the perfect rain-washed air tonight
              and I have no words for him, this
                    enfant terrible / # 2) LINE
                        FROM SUN TO ORBITING BODY
                    SWEEPS OUT EQUAL AREA IN EQUAL TIME /
         geological ages being as difficult to grasp
        as the number of telephone poles/railroad ties/sands
      of the ocean, though Archimedes calculated these down to a grain,
imagine being silent, voiceless, without hearing, hungry, learning
        to hunt by stealth in dark waters / are we still one person?
        will you take off your clothes? taste clear
              liquor from curved leaf, touch
                    tongue to petals, rape/pillage,
                        press into the Real
                    into the crumbling bark of the tree /
        # 3) PLANETARY SPEED VARIES WITH DISTANCE /
We commune tonight, my soul. Take. Eat.

This is our body. This is who we are.

And the enormous trunk sways minutely in response to the weight of its limbs.

Dream of the deep root / *FATHER EDWARD GREENOUGH, 1927* /

Ordovician / FIFTEEN BILLION YEARS OR SO . . . /

We know each other.

11.

To speak of griefs untold /

MERCURY THE MESSENGER

POCKMARKED BY MUSICIANS AND

ARTISTS, DÜRER, BEETHOVEN, MATISSE,

ORBITING AT 48 KM/SEC, WINGED SNAKE ON A STICK /

oiled skin, muscles gliding like steel, overhead

trees shaggy, garroulous as mummers, things of the earth /

AQUILINE ZEZZA / lady, where are you lady tonight? /

AIR 78% NITROGEN (WE DON'T THINK OF THAT

REMEMBERING ONLY THE OXYGEN) WEIGHING

ONE SHORT TON OR 15 LBS/SQ INCH

AT SEA LEVEL, EQUATED

TO SOUL/BREATH/WIND BY GREEKS

SWIRLED BY CORIOLIS, ROTATION /

a troubador came singing

under the greenwood tree /

THYMINE binds quarks into neutrons/protons, strings of no color

because triad must be tricolor, exceptions deteriorating

into electrons and particles / CHILDREN OF LEDA,

CASTOR AND POLLUX, OF WHOM MUCH

POETRY / gluons (glue-ons?)

who says physicists don't

have any fun? Always spin 1 /

singing a soft, enchanting song,

never a care had he . . . /

JOHN THE BAPTIST BORN, AND HELEN KELLER. BENJAMIN

FRANKLIN'S KITE (1752) AND FAST TO RELIEVE DROUGHT IN

MASSACHUSETTS (1749), ROUSSEAU 1712 /

Valves and tubules pumping air and blood
to all organs in complete health--I want you
lady, tonight, these arms lack
arms around them--
earth cannot have us, the sky's
our private dreaming place, dance
of the solstice, perfumed air encouraging lovemaking,
time of the first fruits / the strong force /
PENTECOST OVERWITH, DISCIPLES GET ON WITH IT, TREELIMBS
SWOLLEN AFTER BLOSSOMING, THE ROSENBERGS
EXECUTED 1953 AND LOU GEHRIG HIT FOUR
HOMERUNS / languages surround us
yet we listen only for the human
which is impoverished,
unlike water on rock, birdsong
or windsong in treelimbs and the almost
imperceptible harmonic vibration earth makes
in response to gravity / cloudchamber snailtrails
the only proof they exist / a balladeer came sauntering
loose in his human clothes,
and sang a tender, hungry song
for every broken rose . . .
if you lie still w/o breathing
it enters you.

12.

LEONARD CORNFIELD, 1948
planted by the county, his cronies, old
drinking buddies buried here also, the name
is wistful, portentous, though it raises no face, we wonder,
turning it over in our minds walking under thick shade past so many names /
counting, perhaps the oldest human activity, to measure
with eye, or a stick/standard, to build uniformly
older than prehistory though Egypt
lays claim at 3,000 B.C. naturally /

29

                                    such stuff as dreams
                              are made uf, billy--and our
                        little lives folded into the flux . . . /
                  humerus (ain't it?), deltoid to shoulderbone
            and biceps brachii and brachialis, (triceps brachii
      and auconeus greek gods for all we know), 19 muscles
            to move wrist and fingerbones / *Thales of Miletus*
                  and Pythagoras, the number worshipper, boosted it up
                        one quantum leap into geometry, "The
                              Elements" of Euclid good for a
                                    thousand years /
                              peony bushes after hard rain,
                        petals broken, cupping waterbeads,
                  grandmother (Father's side) brought armloads of them
            into the kitchen to clip and arrange in the chinese vase /
ADENINE hole in the skull (foramen magnum) pointed down for upright walking,
            first toolmakers, meat-eaters, Taung baby found by Dart,
                  and Brook for the adult skulls, five years chiseling
                        free from breccia, australopithecus /
                              the dirt road and worn curbstones,
                                    darkness of spruces,
                              we live on so many levels
                        mixing our metaphors, textures
            of stone and grass, time to lay down among them,
            the afternoon salvaged from work at the office, hunger
for someone to love, someone to give a damn / *Al Khowarizimi, 820 a.d.*
            fathered the algebra, Napier the logarithm and no one knows which
                  Hindu was enlightened by the Zero, ten-based
                        basis for better counting, Leibniz and
                              Newton squabbling over fluxions /
                                    Paranthropus competitor
                              never chipped stone, grubbed,
                        pushed out of food zones, another
            Indian war / What has changed, anyway?
            Strawberries are ready to pick. Midsummer's Eve. Sweet peas bloom.
Man, woman, fit for each other beneath full moon, walk in the yard
            without clothes on--who is to care?--one day in the life--do you

                                    30

                    understand anything at all? Of course.
                        You abound in truth / metacarpals &
                            phalanges gripping stone
                                to strike stone /
                            reducing it all to number,
                    the made thing, perfect science, puzzles
                from flatland, conundrums, chessgames, possibilities
        without risk until $E=MC^2$ *combined with Hiroshima /*
how to live on the planet . . . we dance and dream
            under the full moon, forgetting (for a moment at least)
                the garbage, the sewage of existence, oceans poisoned,
                    ah, what the hell? / discovered by
                            accident, pure luck, in Olduvai
                                Gorge, poking among rocks.

                        13.

                            It is all gesture and signal.
                        Wink of eye, catching movement peripherally
                the eagle finds the fieldmouse, man the woman,
        each sex flirting with visual/audible/tactile/bodylanguage,
even the housefly with its thousand eyes, contracting paramecia, leaves
        (for Chrissake--flowers responding to sunlight) even the soil
                finally sentient, aware of pressure/presence.
                        No signal too subtle to be missed--
                            ask a married man--we are
                                bound to each other /
                    ANTONIO VIVALDI, 37 YEARS
                AT THE OSPEDALE TEACHING YOUNG GIRLS
            AND MOZART (A MASON MIT EIN ZAUBERFLÖTE) WHO DIED
        WITHOUT FRIENDS OR FANFARE, BURIED IN A MASS GRAVE, PAUPER /
GUANINE   Sunday morning just after sunrise, long rays sorted by branches,
            leaves incandescent, leading up into darkness, blue shadows
                broken by dazzling patches, and the heat already
                    welling up out of the grass. I am
                        alive. This moment--alive.
                            Walking in sunlight.
                        31

There is nothing more to it,
days filled with echoes of other days,
remembrance like a holy spirit overshadowing it all /
A FRIEND TO FRIENDS, THE GOD OF THE GATHAS, AHURA MAZDA /
AND IN AMONGST THE USUAL WARS OF THE PERIOD, A GRABBAG OF INTELLECTS:
GOETHE, KANT, JOHNSON AND BOSWELL, NOT TO MENTION ROUSSEAU
WITH HIS "NOBLE SAVAGE" BULLSHIT FIRING THE IMAGINATION
FROM WHICH PROCEEDS BOATLOADS OF SOON-TO-BE
DISAPPOINTED ARISTOCRATS OFF
FOR THE WILDERNESS
TO BE SCALPED BY THE IROQUOIS /
We accept 99.9% of all that occurs
without question or conscious awareness, entering
the stairway of color, crystal pattern of variations
huge and resonant, fed by retina, hammer/stirrup/anvil, sensors
in skin and hair, nostril, tympan, all of it chemical,
shooting through cellwall to the brain in primordial
darkness save where sunlight penetrates bone
and we call it Reality /
GREATEST EVIL IS
FALSEHOOD/HYPOCRISY/CHEATING
THE PROPHET MARTYRED, LIGHT VS DARK,
GREATEST GOOD IN PURITY OF THOUGHT OF ACTION /
All living a form of artwork, artifice but not artificial
except with the beginner who cannot make but must copy signals of others
and even their mimicry is genuine in nature, the hand
shaping clay pot, basket, chiseling the war canoe
or scraping quill across vellum, brushes
of horsehair, whittling our gods
out of scraps chosen
for their particular difference
(a signal) lending to decoration and the
mind seeking out form, exploring possibility always
inventive, creative, God's image in us, eternal child /
VENDIDAD, AND THE ZEND-AVESTA, SACRED TO PARSIS AND GHEBERS TO THIS DAY
EVEN THE SINNERS ARE SAVED EVENTUALLY / the door opens

into gardens invisible without flesh, deoxyribonucleic
ladders through protoplasm with elegant
backspin and bodyenglish, ah
jesus, it delights me /
A TURNING POINT, THE THREE
REVOLUTIONS, GREATEST OF WHICH BEING
INDUSTRIAL, BLASTFURNACES AND WROUGHT IRON BRIDGES
ENDING THE AGE OF KINGS ON THE PENPOINTS OF BOURGOISE MERCHANTS /
gestures most simple and natural the best--handshake, smile, waving goodbye
or the tear glimmering eyelash, red flags waving love from the
rooftops, barricades in the streets, one finger
is worth a thousand words / leading to
endings, beginnings, ongoings
and *FINIS BENTLEY*
whose name is poetically apt
in this place, where we all are ignorant
yet delight in invention, each madman in his corner,
the combined cacophony closest to what we call God (author
of images, splitter of prisms) so that even this unstructured act of walking
in sunlight on Sunday without a thought about sin or confession
or anything religious becomes an act of pure
worship to Thou, whatever Your Name,
surrounding in darkness or light
I say Halleluhia
(why shouldn't I?) just for the
hell of it--for myself and for everyone
buried/unburied (even for you, old G.F.H.)
Hell yes--Halleluhia! / *ARMED WITH THEIR SCIENCE, WITH MAPS*
THEY SET OFF TO EXPLORE ICEFLOWS AND JUNGLES, MEN IN SMALL SHIPS MEASURING
STARLIGHT, CROSSING INVISIBLE LINES ON THE EARTH, FINDING
NEW WORLDS AND SUBDUING THEM VIGOROUSLY,
ALL IN THE NAME OF . . .

14.

ADENINE THE BODY TWO-THIRDS
SALTWATER COVERING 2/3 EARTH'S
SURFACE AND THE SUN ENTERING CANCER, MOON
IS OUR SYMBOL THIS MONTH WHEN JON AND I ARE BORN /
A season of grass, thick as a pelt, walking barefoot to feel the resiliant
soil, network of spiders, ants traversing long blades carrying
wingbits, serrated edges, everything particular down to
the finest detail, loose trees call to me
beckoning darkness / *equal volumes*
of two gasses contain the
same number of molecules at equal
temperature and pressure, Amedeo (Love of God)
Avogardro / PRAESEPE THE BEEHIVE CONTAINED IN IT ALSO
TIDES PULLED BY THE GODDESS RISING 50 MIN LATER EACH NIGHT, MARE
TRANQUILLITAS, MARE HUMORUM, MARE FECUNDITATIS, TYCHO
AND SIX DAYS AFTER HIS BIRTH, MEN SETTING FOOT

ON THE TRANQUIL SEAS TO SEE EARTH FOR
THE FIRST TIME ISOLATE/LOVELY /
How do I measure it? Each time
walking here (earthworm
nibbling through darkness, paired
butterflies waltzing over the graves) knowing
what I know (and cannot know) about living and dying
about your life and death, parents, grandmother, gone from me
now over a decade and the upswelling curl of my own death unimaginable
like a wave that has travelled for thousands of miles crashing now on my face,
water in bark, pressure in tubules, suction, resuction, tidal,
we are made of water, e.g. the dead squirrel flattened
by traffic dehydrated, blowing away / *extraction*
of copper from malachite somewhere in
Persia 5000 B.C. and bronze
by 3800, better
weaponry, decorated bells of
the Shang Dynasty peak of the artwork
and Samurai sword, steel the ultimate alchemy
folding layer on layer for flexible strength out of fire /
If we miss a stitch now and again, what then? Irregularity is God's
mark of perfection / POTATOES CAME TO EUROPE (SWIMMING?) 1586
AND ICE CREAM CONE INTRODUCED IN ST. LOUIS 1904 /
fascination with names and numbers, marks cut in
time cut in stone, even *HARRY SPEED* stuck
in the open field where the county
buries the paupers, has a
name and a number
(think of him moving through
time like a baseball's path in slow-
motion high speed film starting between some
woman's legs emerging screaming to curve through space
and end up in Pocatello, Idaho under a flat stone 1958 / *Democritus*
first saw Reality/atoms in empty space/from which J. Dalton and Mendeleev's table
of weights and measures / NAMED FOR THE CRAB WHO MOVES
FORWARD AND BACKWARD WITH US IN ITS CLAW /

35

Loafing in the long grass in summer heat on Sunday
afternoon, sprawled out by the stone of
CATHERINE RICH who is rich no
longer, watching spiders
and ants, aware of all that is not
me, of movement in space at this moment on all
sides of amazing creatures, oblivious of my seemingly
godlike presence above them, each with its work, and how
artificial the manmade world appears, asphalt bubbling in sunlight
sticking to tires of unending vehicles, aluminum/chromium fenders/antennae
and radios, lawnmowers chattering, powersaws, intrusive pulse
of electrical noise hammering in and around consciousness
so we are never free of it, even in wilderness
the jet roaring overhead marking the sky
and sometimes I get so damned
tired of it all
I almost envy these sleepers /
AND THEY SHOT THE CZAR AND HIS FAMILY
THIS MONTH, 1918 / trees in full leaf
and apples forming, some things immeasureable, five
crows in the branches, darkness under grass, between galaxies . . .

15.

"STARS IN MYRIADS, WHICH HAVE NEVER BEEN SEEN BEFORE AND WHICH SURPASS THE OLD,
PREVIOUSLY KNOWN, STARS IN NUMBER MORE THAN TEN," SIDEREUS
NUNCIUS, 1610, A SHORT, SQUARE, ACTIVE MAN WITH RED
HAIR, POWER HEIGHTENED TO 30X, AND THE MOON:
"IT IS A MOST BEAUTIFUL AND
DELIGHTFUL SIGHT" /
Panic creeps in at
the edges.   Forty years old
and what to show for it all? Moving
air riffles through grave grass, touching each blade /
FIRST LAND ANIMALS MILLIPEDS AND SCORPIONS / there is
great work being done in nuclear physics/great work in biochemistry /
NINE SPHERES FORMING OUT OF THE GAS CLOUDS, SIX ROTATING COUNTERCLOCKWISE, DUST

BLOWN OFF BY SOLAR WIND WHEN THE SUN IGNITED (6 BILLION OR SO B.C.)
CODEX 1181 POPE URBAN VIII, PROPOSITIONS TO BE FORBIDDEN:
THAT THE SUN IS IMMOVEABLE AT THE CENTRE OF THE
HEAVENS, THAT THE EARTH IS NOT THE CENTRE
AND IS NOT IMMOVEABLE, ETC . . ./
The air I breathe this day
no less pure than any before me, they
put their pants on one leg at a time, do not
have any more fingers or eyes (forget Chagall's artist)
and will, as the Preacher saith, be gone tomorrow to the same
place (what is that place?) with the fools and the presidents, even the
poor possess their own bodies, have moments of utter privacy which cannot be known
and so why this continual anxiety THYMINE about achievement? Can we
unravel the code of the galaxies and live one day longer?
Vanity of vanities (pull down thy vanity--e.p.)
the great double helix unraveled and
then what? / DOMINANT PREDATOR WATER
SCORPIONS NINE FEET LONG /
Why do I write poetry and not music
not quantum mechanics or astrological forecasts?
Great work to be done in Africa, Dr. Schweitzer /
MAFFEO BARBERINI WITH HIS FOOT ON THE OLD MAN'S NECK AFTER
THE TRIAL 1633--DO NOT CROSS ME AGAIN, YOU DAMNED GENIUS--BECAUSE
DIALOGUE ON THE GREAT WORLD SYSTEMS SNOOKERED THE CENSORS, MADE THE INDEX FOR
SEVERAL CENTURIES AT LEAST, AND G. WRITING OUT IN HIS OWN HAND:
"I, GALILEO GALILEI, SON ON VINCENZO GALILEI, FLORENTINE,
AGED SEVENTY YEARS . . . SWEAR THAT I HAVE ALWAYS
BELIEVED, DO NOW BELIEVE, AND BY GOD'S
HELP WILL ALWAYS . . . WHATEVER
YOU WANT, MASSA /
I want to burn and flare and be
consumed to a fine, white ash /
SHALLOW SEAS, LOW CONTINENTS, FISH AND CORALS FOR
TWENTY MILLION YEARS, BUT WHERE ARE THEY NOW? CRUMBLING AWAY
AT 9,425 FEET ABOVE SEA LEVEL SOMEWHERE IN UTAH / name in cut stone:
JOHN P. ANASTASOPOULOUS 1855-1925, something to outlast flesh, we act in a hall

37

of mirrors, thoughts long in forming hang from our fingers, backward
and forward, none of them visible, repeating the pattern,
stones that have waited ten millennia
for our names . . .

16.

The hand on the cave wall,
outlined with ochre, the flesh
deteriorates, cancer in the family, life
expectancy a roll of the dice, law of averages good
only for insurance companies, not subject to war or
high speed vehicles, not applicable in specific cases,
my children, your children, the face of my wife which I have come
to love, lying beside her in soft light of morning, the sheets rumpled, how calm
and beautiful it seems to be completely relaxed and breathing /
three spin one vector bosons carry the weak force /
a grubber, basically--vegetarian--with
large grinding molars, the skull almost
gorilla-like, big fellows--
around 140 lbs /
affects all matter particles,
but not force-carrying particles, carry
100 GeV mass at low energies, responsible for
radioactive decay, Salam & Weinberg, 1967 / smoky darkness
flickering torchlight, bison & antelope & the small stick-figured men
hunting with spears translates into the Velvet Girl half naked on a billboard,
skepticism our watermark, bring no sentiments forward unless
you are religious--and then you can be ignored /
Paranthropus, competitor not ancestor /
Ah, well, science is lacking
in that it cares little for
poetry/music/magic
the hand on the cave wall
except as a curiosity to be examined
numerically, huge machines grinding forth gathering grain

38

instead of the sickle lined with obsidian flakes, my purpose
complete now that I have fathered children, raised them to maturity /
footprints left in soft ash at Olduvai CYTOSINE W plus, W minus and Z naught
behave similarly to photons at high energy / so my son
came into the light on Bastille Day at around 9 a.m.
I will never forget looking out that window
after seeing his smashed-in face so
beautiful red blackhaired
and boisterous--
Jesus! that's what it's all about!
Now I can follow the others, skull washed loose
in the creekbed, fingerbones sifted from sand, chiseled
from breccia, nameless and faceless, signposts, *WING SONG 1928*,
hand-made gravestones inlaid with mother-of-pearl, finger-formed concrete,
hand on the cave wall, spraypainted on brickwalls, Kilroy was here . . .

17.

What I cannot accomplish, another will perform.
What I create, fulfills another's dream. The tiny points
radiate in all directions, waves of the soul /
HEAR O ISRAEL, THE LORD OUR GOD, THE LORD IS ONE /
seat of compassion throughout literature,
where if we did not suck
we snuzzled, comforted by softness,
contrasted with Bruce Lee's bursting pectorals
straited musculature, throacic bodybuilding /
YA THE UNNAMEABLE, THE DEMANDING, GOD OF WILDERNESS
PILLAR OF FIRE AND SMOKE, BROODING IN DARKNESS, THOU SHALT HAVE NO
OTHER GODS BEFORE ME, CECIL B. DEMILLE PRODUCTION WITH CASTS OF THOUSANDS CANNOT
EVEN COME CLOSE TO THE TERRIBLE MYSTERY, CHERUBIM AND SEPAPHIM
FANNING HIM WITH WINGS, WHO BURNED BEFORE MOSES
AND DOES NOT LIVE IN OBJECTS OR NEED
SACRIFICE / tell me your stories, stones--
here are men I would have loved--
women to fall in love with--

39

children like my own children,
wells of continual delight--surely all
varieties lie under this grass--musicians, philosophers,
characters of all sorts THYMINE bronchia to bronchioles,
alveoli (600 million of them in each of us) clustered into
lobules pink with blood at firstbreath, blackened by lifetime
of filtering atmosphere, capturing particles with
cillia lining all passages / I am a poet,
born this month, this week, at noon,
my gift to speak with honesty,
tempering emotion while the
spirit rages,
touching the wordless ones
who dance while I have no coordination,
who surround me with food, protect me from harm,
the epitaph reads: here lies one part of all that lives forever /
THE TORAH HIS BOOK, PENTATEUCH AND PROPHETS, SHULHAN ARUK THE REGULATIONS
DOCUMENTING MISHNAH AND GEMARA, MEZUZAH OVER LINTEL, TEFILLIN ON FOREHEAD,
TALLIT OVER THE SHOULDERS IN PRAYER, FOLLOWING THE CANTOR /
diaphragm pulling in pushing out, pleura
protecting and the hard sternum that has to be
sawed apart in surgery splitting
the cage / KADDISH SUNG FOR
THE DEAD, GREAT YAHWEH
RECEIVE INTO YOUR HANDS THIS SPIRIT,
ELOI, ELOI, ADONAI, ELOHIM, NONE OF THEM
GOD'S NAME HE IS HAGGIOS, HOLY, SEPARATE FROM US
UTTERLY OTHER / all this in darkness fighting off depression
because I am middle-aged and have found no greatness, questioning
why I seek greatness when so many have lived and died without it, why I should not
want only a Kaddish to be sung over me, someone to mourn for a little,
someone I don't know to walk by my gravestone and wonder
about me, as I ask privately of *ORANGE LEMON*
1879-1941 what could you tell me
that I need to know, oh
tell me quickly /

TISHAH B'AB, FAST DAY
COMMEMORATING DESTRUCTION OF TEMPLES
(ONE BY BABYLONIAN, THE SECOND BY TITUS IN 70 A.D.)
DISPERSING THY PEOPLE THROUGH EUROPE TO SUFFER, JEHOVAH THY
WILL IS DIFFICULT TO KEEP, THY THRONE UNAPPROACHABLE, SPRINKLE LAMB'S
BLOOD ON THE ALTAR, TWO HUNDRED THOUSAND SHEEP AND DOVES KEPT FOR THE KILLING BY
THE TIME OF JESUS (YAHSHUA, YAHWEH IS SALVATION) WHO STEPPED OVER
KIDRON STREAM RUNNING BLOODRED AT PASSOVER INTO THE
GARDEN FOR ONE LAST WRESTLE WITH YOU.

18.

To bring forth your own kind,
to care for your own kind,
both child and elderly,
investing your hours in their lives,
tending as the good husbandman tends his trees,
both parents together needed for this, both
investing their hours, morning and evening, listening, teaching
and just being around to admire, even to scold, to be involved
so that the child knows boundaries, knows where he/she belongs, feels secure
as I felt sitting on mother's lap while she lulled me a song,
or on father's strong knee while he read stories,
in this we participate with all others, animal and
human alike, with God in His mystery
who brings us forth creative
to care for each other /
LE ROI S'EN, LOUIS 14, CROMWELL
STILL IN POWER, THOUGH CHARLES COMING, END
OF THE TURKISH INVASIONS, AUSTRIANS KEEPING'EM OUT OF
VIEN, GOD IN HIS IMMACULATE REASON WINDING THE UNIVERSE TIGHT
AS A SWISS WATCH / I mothered four children, lost one to measles, one
to whooping cough, one died of her first and the last buried me / *JEWS BURNED*
BY THE INQUISITION, SEPHARDIC NOBILITY PUSHED OUT OF SPAIN, BURNED
ALSO IN FRANKFURT 1614 THE WHOLE GHETTO BLAZING /
leaving our old ones to die in those places

                    "the final solution" to the

                        geriatric problem, never acceptable /

                    GUANINE Worked every day

                of my life since I can remember,

            on the farm and later in the silver mines,

        had my head busted a few times, never thought where the

    next meal was coming from, up early each day ready for action /

    neglect of our own flesh and blood is a great sin, no matter

what we might say in defense of it, all the good reasons, in the end we know

    heartache and guilt, anguish, dilemma and there are no answers save to

        suffer and serve each other, that's why we're here /

                Parents from Athens, landed Ellis Island,

                    took train out here to make fortune except

                        they made no fortune, only a

                            living, had seven

                        children including myself,

                    stones carved in Greek because we have not

            forgotten where we come from / *ASHKENAZIC "JUDISCH"*

    LOOKING TO SABBATAI ZEVA WHO PLAYED THE MESSIAH ALL OVER EUROPE

UNTIL THE SULTAN TOOK HIM FROM SMYRNA TO BECOME MEHEMED EFFENDI (1663)

OR LOSE HIS HEAD, SO GOES THE OLD BALL GAME / Came out with the Cavalry

        to fight old Joseph, retired and settled, buried before

            they had stonecutters, wooden slab gone /

                    JESUS ORESCO saw light, drew breath, heard voice

                    without understanding, felt love

                    without understanding,

                        clung to it

                    till the cold darkness came /

            And if you don't participate--if each of us

            doesn't participate, caring for children and animals,

        nurturing trees, tying the sweet peas, spading the soil with

    manure and last years leaves--if we ignore it and go for the quick buck

then the skies will evaporate over our heads, and the firestorms burn us to death

    as the untended earth and her children claim their Shabbat /

        PURE REASON THE LATEST CRAZE, NEWTON BENDING LIGHT

                                42

WHILE LIEBNIZ PARSED THE UNIVERSE INTO MONADS
AND HOBBES' ACCURATE OBSERVATION ON
THE HUMAN CONDITION PLAYING
OFF J. SWIFT'S
MODEST PROPOSAL, MEANTIME SPINOZA
ENTERS THE MIND OF THE ALMIGHTY AND LIVES THERE /
We fight you still, resist still, will not be
dominated or transformed. There are gods older than your
white god, powers that will not bend to bibles, the People survive /
That morning I saw you, daughter, our firstborn, fingers curled by the halo of
your hair, my heart melted and I wept, knowing I would do anything
for you, holding you small, contained and safe in the
hollow of my arm, rocking until we both slept,
these changes are chemical, larger than intellect,
perfectly natural, our birthright,
bonded together.

19.

TAUGHT HIMSELF MATH IN THE
PLAGUE YEARS, 1665-1666, LIGHT SPLITTER
BORN CHRISTMAS DAY, UNLOVED, UNABLE TO LOVE SAVE
NUMBERS, THEIR COMBINATIONS, FLUXIONS HE CALLED THEM, ISOLATE
"I PROCURED ME A TRIANGULAR GLASS-PRISME, TO TRY THEREWITH THE
CELEBRATED PHAENOMENA OF COLOURS" / systolic, diastolic, back & forth,
tidal pressures 120/min in youth, extending to 70/min in the
mature creature, noticeable in third month, tied
to the mother, her rhythm, moon and sea /
Endless, wind in summer leaves, harvest
of lives, songs in the air,
some a few hours,
others a century, some with
religion, others without thought or light,
diverse as molecular combinations, mixtures of history,
none better than another, all compelling, I won't claim originality
but follow Edgar, Walter, Thornton, others / CROSSOPTERYGII HAD JAWS

43

AND AIR BLADDERS (PRECURSOR OF LUNGS, 405 M. B.C.) ANCESTOR TO FROG, SALAMANDER /
Left only the Wall standing (Titus, 70 a.d.) where the devout stand
touching lips to blocks carved by Solomon's stonecutters,
shoving paper prayers into the cracks/black
granite with chiseled names reflecting
faces in tears in prayer /
pericardium
walls dividing into chambers
at six weeks, evolves through fish &
frog, then snake, turtle, the human totem of
forms and faces, 200 million years coming together
in superior vena cava, inferior vena cava, atrium, ventricle
semilunar, tricuspid, mitral, the foramen ovale closing after birth
and the priest lifts it out still beating O sacred
heart of Jesus framed on the wall / CALCULATED MOTION
OF MOON AROUND EARTH, "I DEDUCED THAT THE FORCES
WHICH KEEP THE PLANETS IN THEIR ORBS
MUST BE RECIPROCALLY AS THE
SQUARES OF THEIR
DISTANCES FROM THE CENTRES
ABOUT WHICH THEY REVOLVE" / That first winter
I came here daily, wrestling with loneliness, exile in a
cold country, grabbed hold of those huge cottonwoods that swayed
like ancestral gods above the Japanese stones, pressed my face like a
prayer into the cracks in the bark, crying Lord, Lord . . . / ORA BUFFALOE 1896-
1936 / TREES APPEAR, EVERGREENS AND FERNS, AND THE LAND KNOWS
SPIDERS AND THE FIRST TRUE INSECTS / Their elegant
stones in a lovely quarter where the road
curves, Taoistic simplicity, generating
peace ADENINE and the Greeks
with oval ceramic
photographs, inscriptions in
demotic, Aegean homeland echoed in Idaho /
THAT PRIMAL DISC EMERGING 5 BILLION YEARS TO IGNITION
AT 15 M KELVINS IN THE CORE, ENGINE DRIVING LIFE OUT OF SOIL,
YOU CAN FEEL IT STEAMING OVER THE FIELDS ON A SUMMER MORNING, A GOD

IF THERE EVER WAS ONE WORTHY OF NAMING RE, RA, SOL, SOUL OF ALL WORSHIP, ADONIS
AND THE SPICULES SHOOT UP IN GREAT ARCS VISIBLE IN ECLIPSE
WHEN THE GREAT CORONA PULSATES, COOKING THE SOUP /
and back of it all, discovered one afternoon, along
a fencerow overgrown with summer vines, the
gate, half open, half broken down,
to let you out simply
into the natural chaos of grass and bushes,
milkweed, thistles, clotting the irrigation ditch,
the disorganized universe that is always there for us,
despite our organization, where the grass grows deep as
the 19th century, Walter, it is your gate / MECHANICS OF LIGHT,
MECHANICS OF MOVING BODIES, THE METAL UNIVERSE OILED AND CLICKING LIKE CLOCKS /
where the dead arrive in formal style, through the silver horse-
shoe masonic arch, and escape naked as wind, barefoot,
through this half-hidden gentle gate,
leaving nothing behind but their names . . .

20.

AGE OF REASON BE DAMNED.
AGE OF REVOLUTION, REFORMATION
AND 10,000 HUGUENOTS TORN LIMB FROM LIMB
IN THAT MOST CIVILIZED MADHOUSE, PARIS, AUGUST 1572
WHICH MASSACRE NAMED FOR ST. BARTHOLEMEW WAS TOASTED
BY CROWNED HEADS INCLUDING PHILLIP OF SPAIN (MOST CATHOLIC MONARCH)
AND POPE GREGORY XIII IN A SPECIAL THANKSGIVING MASS, HEADS AND
GENITALS HOISTED ON PIKES, AUSCHWITZ HAS NOTHING ON ATROCITY, CROMWELL INKING
THE MOST CIVILIZED LEGAL HEADCHOPPING OF CHARLES FOR THE GOOD OF
HUMANITY, ETC. MURDER UNENDING, 30 YEARS WAR, THERE ARE
NO NEW TORTURES / This the sun's season,
dog days and dryness come to fields, ruling and
management are the skills, myself, born
on the cusp, destined
to be an actor or a king, and the nights
stay warm until midnight, we sit on the patio drinking

45

                wine and smoking cigars and talking in the moonlight,
          sweetness in air and no thought for mortality or the coming winter /
        REGULUS IS DOMINANT IN LEO, THIS MONTH JESUS WAS
    TRANSFIGURED AND JOHN BEHEADED, BEGIN CANNING GARDEN VEGETABLES,
        IN LOUISIANA THEY BLESS THE SHRIMP FLEET, MOTHER ANN
        LEE ARRIVED IN N.Y. 1774 AND SPUTNIK SHOT TWO
                DOGS INTO SPACE 1960 (I WAS IN HIGH SCHOOL AND
                    REMEMBER THE PANIC), VEGA GLEAMS IN LYRA
                        AND ALTAIR IN AQUILA, THE
                            PERSEIDS SCRIBE THE HEAVENS
                        AND IN THE SOUTHWEST, ANTARES /
                Master yourself before you would master others,
            the leader always going into battle first, you cannot
          push string (Eisenhower), and no one respects cowards or sluggards,
      responsibility prods the ordinary to rise to the occasion, as in
  track in my senior year (I was no star athlete) made co-captain, I did more
      leg-lifts and push-ups than anyone thought possible leading the
            others, not wanting to let them down / Mushrooms sprout
                in the shadow of stones. I ride my bicycle
                through the network of leaves in
                    coolness CYTOSINE thinking of
                        BERTHA GRUNDY 1880-1926
                    her life and times / *THIRD CHILD BORN TO*
              JOHN AND MARY, BAPTIZED (WE BELIEVE) APRIL
              26, 1564, HE FATHERED THREE CHILDREN ABANDONED LATER
          AND WROTE TWO PLAYS/YEAR FOR WHICH WE FORGIVE HIM ALL ERRORS /
        LEO'S BEING FORCEFUL, GENEROUS AND WELL-ORGANIZED BASTARDS,
    COMPATIBLE WITH ARIES (THANK GOD), CONSUMING AS FIRE CONSUMES
        AND TRANSFORMS INTO HEAT/LIGHT/ENERGY THE BODY, CONFUCIUS
            BORN 551 B.C. AND FRANS HALS DEPARTING 1666 /
                the good king, good parent, works tirelessly
                    on behalf of others, spends little
                        on personal luxury, lives
                            sacrificially, not
                        striving for honors but to be
                happily remembered   / MUIGEL BORN ALSO

                                46

IN THIS AGE OF SLAUGHTER, SOLDIER, WOUNDED AT LEPANTO
IN THE ARMADA OF DON JUAN (1571) AND SOLD LATER INTO SLAVERY BY
BARBARY CORSAIRS, ROTTED IN ALGIERS FIVE YEARS TILL HIS MOTHER RANSOMED
HIS CRIPPLED BONES AND FINALLY, AFTER FIFTY YEARS OF RELATIVE POVERTY, WROTE
IN PRISON FOR DEBT, THAT MASTERPIECE OF WINDMILLS AND DREAMING,
REMBRANDT ALSO A DEBTOR, PAINTING DARK PORTRAITS,
AND THEY CALL IT AN AGE OF REASON / MONEY, LIKE MANURE,
MUST BE SPREAD AROUND, AND HE WHO FALLS IN LOVE
WITH HIMSELF WILL HAVE NO RIVALS . . .

21.

The grass is dry now,
thin to the touch. Trees spew out their
seeds and spiders hang in hammocks. How many life-
times are ahead of us? / COSMO TODERO, BORN IN
RIPPABOTON, ITALY 1889 ADENINE fascination with chipped stone,
squatting for hours in the sunlight, smacking one to another,
learning the touch of the grain / RIG VEDA, SAMA VEDA, YAJUR VEDA, ATHARVA VEDA
EACH TRIPARTITE (SAMHITAS, BRAHMANAS, UPANISHADS) AND THE CODE
OF MANU LAYING DOWN THE CASTE SYSTEM, FROM BEFORE WORDS
BEFORE BOOKS, THESE STORIES / and societies
of hunters, colored mud, bones
strung with sinews to hang around neck
and colored pebbles
telling of power, the long stick
whipped through air burying stonepoint /
and each day brings its work, rising out of bed to fix
something to eat, putting on clothes, then hours occupied with
labor, bringing income, bread, money, barter, trade, wealth, whatever it
translates into, back to the home, hustling together in harmony with fellows
at this workplace or that, forgetting how unnatural it is
to live in concrete and glass, be paid with paper
or numbers and seldom (never?) stand alone
in a grove of trees or grass plain
unprotected with nothing
particular to do /

47

                   carnivore--broke bone to eat marrow /
           BRAHMA   CREATOR, VISHNU PRESERVER, SHIVA DESTROYER
        ALL BORN OUT OF BRAHMAN, THIS TRINITY A DREAM IN THE MIND OF A GOD
         LIKE THE MILKY WAY SPREAD OUT ACROSS THE HEAVENS ON A SUMMER NIGHT
    AN ORDERING OF LIGHTS, WORLDSYSTEM IMPENETRABLE, CHANGING ALWAYS / on the plains
            of east Africa 1 M b.c. this smaller, more clever (nastier)
               meat-eater drove off the root-grubber, drove them
                   like hells angels at a church picnic /
                    strong dominating weak, each seeking
                       the proper level, rebellion
                         never far below the surface,
                      the soul with its secret, sharpened knife /
                 ARJUNA AND KRISHNA BEFORE THE BATTLE:
              SHOW ME THE FACE OF GOD. YOU CANNOT STAND TO SEE IT.
             SHOW ME ANYWAY. AND KRISHNA REVEALING HIS MANIFOLD FEATURES
         MORE BLINDING THAN DIRECT SUNLIGHT SWARMING WITH IMAGES / Remembrance
    is artwork, the carved stick or little chiseled goddess not important to everyday
            foodgathering, hunting, killing--the decorated bowl common as
                grainhusks--poem and song passed down in the quiet evening--
                these shards are all that remain after flesh
                   and the complete person, unknown,
                       slips into the darkness /
                         EACH ACTION
                      INFLUENCES THE SOUL
                   WHICH NEVER DIES BUT IS REBORN
                 TO THE YOKE OF ITS KARMA / most live in their clutter,
             broken shoes, broken furniture permeated with that particular
          odor/aroma/scent of the foxden, live surrounded by things, artifacts
     gathered from days of years, caches of memory, touchstones, toys that sustain us
         and which, when we are dead, become useless junk to be hauled away
                like they cleaned out Aunt Bea's ocean cottage (three
                   days it took them using a front-end loader)
                      the young couple who bought it began
                         cleaning thoroughly every trace
                            of her effluvia
                         from woodwork and glass,

                                  48

transforming the shell into a new foxden
to fill with their own quirky artifacts which another
couple in fifty years will trash with amused wonder / standing
erect in small groups yowling after a kill or a raid for females,
curved sticks shaken in air, comes man the destroyer the death the end of the
perfectly ordered world with its efficient silence, nameless
they stride from the garden with bloodied fingers /
MAHABHARATA, BHAGDVAD-GITA, RAMAYANA, PURANAS AND
MOKSHA/PERFECTION BEYOND REBIRTH
THAT STRANGE DREAM OF HEAVEN
SOLITARY/STILL
AT THE CENTER OF ALL WHIRLED
DREAMS, THE MASTER SLEEPER / I do not
fear death because no animal fears it . . .

22.

Stones, the wind over them . . . /
To name and classify--that was the task God assigned Adam, curious
what he would call that which he had not created--the act being essentially
human unlike any other creature we count and we name, we establish time
with its segments/fragments of activity/dates cut in stone /
I pretend to be myself, become the lie instead.
What was I but a scaffold for children
and wife to hang from? / "Three Quarks
for Muster Mark" Murray
Gell-Mann named 'em supposedly from
Joyce--how's that fer yer sober scientist? /
Anaximander (500 B.C.) held that man evolved (hear that
Darwin?) from fish because they had lungs. Medicine
began the study, although folk remedies from witch doctors and old wives
named all the useable plants, some sticking to our time despite Linnaeus /
Got rich selling fertilizer. Broke my back hauling railroad
ties. Paid no income tax for fifty-three years. /
Andreas Vesalius 1500 a.d. classified musculature /
The mountain lakes rimmed with snow. /

49

Animacules scurrying in pondwater,
cells of shaved cork-wood,
the Dutchman peering through the other end
of the telescope into the next universe down /
Years of loneliness, married to a stupid man /
which come in six flavors (up, down, strange, charmed, beauty &
((you guessed it)) truth) each of which has three colors /
Thousands of shoes, flapping their tongues at me day and night, brazzle of
stitcher and polishing wheels, the belts humming, wagging
their mocking tongues and broken soles / *Gregor*
Mendel crossing his sweet peas, Burbank his peanuts
and Chas. Darwin leaning over the deckrails,
winged creatures labled and pinned /
THYMINE Saw my first
action at Guadalcanal--scared
the shit outta me / binds protons (2 up, 1 down)
and neutrons (1 up, 2 down) tighter than Elmer's glue,
broke by the queball in accelerator spinning off into sidepocket /
The parties at Dean's house, all those white chiffon lovely little
social-climbing hypocrites / *BESSIE O. BUCKINGHAM SMITH* / Shuttles,
wind noises, leaves over stones, all of them my voice,
imagined, yet the heart hears and separates
naming and classifying / *Watson & Crick, 1953,*
cracked Pandora's cookiejar and
here comes yer cloned
bandersnatch.

23.

oh, that yellow tree
engorged with sun! Standing
beneath it, soaking the bright nimbus into my soul,
dizzy as a monarch's wing / Choukoutien cave 1927 Davidson
Black with one molar definitely human / holds roughly one quart
of masticated mash mixed with pepsin and HCL (to kill microbes)
this bag distends two/five hours or so before undulating

50

peristaltic (20 sec apart) through pylorus into / GREAT
CARBONIFEROUS 345-280 MILLION FERN FORESTS AMID VOLCANOES
INFESTED WITH TWO-FOOT DRAGONFLIES, FLYING BUGS,
BIGGEST MOSQUITO SWAMP IN HISTORY /
CYTOSINE
barefoot on cool, smooth
grainy stone, immortal from toetip
to fingertip reflecting primal light, everything
I see is perfect this afternoon, sun on white marble, seeds
in the air, dragonflies hovering, zipping away / 14 skulls, jaws and
150 teeth assembled into roughly 45 individuals of all ages, also charred bones
and plenty of flaked tools, chipped quartz, chert, fire discovered
possibly in that process 500,000 B.C. / REPTILES
FIRST TO LAY EGGS ON LAND, SAFE FOR
A FEW MILLION YEARS / shall I strip
off my clothes? give in
to my desire?
And why not--all will soon
be dust, ashes, dirt, the rigid dead
surround me on all sides in their soft and gentle
dissolving of problems into sponge of soil, leaftip, blade /
residence of compassion, "in the bowels of Christ I beseech
you," the chyme squirting in to be massaged by a million villi
pulling out chyle through lacteals, twenty feet of it
and the colon another five feet extended / they
spread on foot (good legs for walking) from
Olduvai region across bridges into
Asia and what is now Java /
OCEAN MILLIKEN
SIXTEEN YRS HE CAME HERE /
naked as I am in mind, light sweeping
each inch of me, illuminating tiny hairs, washing
me clean of all death, disease, for this particular instant /
flintworker, firekeeper, hunter of great beasts, mastodon, sabertooth /
AND NOW THEY ARE DIGGING IT ALL OUT TO BE BURNED IN BLAST FURNACES OR TO HEAT THE
HOMES OF THE BOURGEOISE, THREE HUNDRED MILLION YEARS IN FORMING /

jejunum, ileum, haustra coli, sigmoid colon,
cecum, rectum & the rest of it ruler
of all members always ends
up being some old
asshole.

24.

THE GREAT LEARNING
TAKES ROOT IN CLARIFYING THE WAY
WHEREIN THE INTELLIGENCE INCREASES THROUGH
THE PROCESS OF LOOKING STRAIGHT INTO ONE'S OWN HEART
AND ACTING ON THE RESULTS; ROOTED IN WATCHING WITH AFFECTION THE
WAY PEOPLE GROW (E.P. OF KUNG 1928) / sit by the stone of *A.C. WITHERSPOON*,
autumn quickens the air, dryness, a bright color, summer gone
from the spruces in blue fire, the abandoned urn
filled with pine needles: Perpetual care /
IN SIGN OF THE VIRGIN BORN
THIS MONTH, SPICA
HER STAR
THE MILKY WAY TURNING FROM
NORTH TO EAST SLOWLY EACH NIGHT WITH
JUPITER IN THE EAST, VENUS IN WESTERN HORIZON /
The poet's complaint, dated and dogeared. See, the first dry leaves
falling in sharp-edged morning light, crisp on white stone, tips and edges tinged
with yellow, invaded by death in her bright colors that fade into
umber. Time gathers its days. Let loose the drawstring
in your mind. Anxiety collapses like a bag.
In the end there is this hole in the ground,
pile of loose dirt, tin marker,
heap of wilted flowers
and no one after fifty years who
gives a damn / WHEN THINGS HAVE BEEN CLASSIFIED
IN ORGANIC CATEGORIES, KNOWLEDGE MOVES TOWARD FULFILLMENT /
Pray for us now and at the hour of our death / IMAGINE
TEN THOUSAND DEAD OF THE PLAGUE THIS MONTH 1665, OR HANK

52

WILLIAMS BORN WITH JOHNNY APPLESEED, MCKINLEY SHOT AND GERONIMO
COAXED IN OFF THE DESERT 1886, COVER YOUR TOMATOES
AGAINST FIRST FROST / how I enjoy my body,
although I abuse it with too much food,
too little exercise, companion
since first breath, the
richest gift,
good health in all organs,
bowels performing, kidneys doing
their stuff daily without pain and heart
continuing to lub-dub/lub-dub like a jogger around the
track of days and years so I need to prepare myself for the end
which cannot be imagined or believed in / 551 B.C. KUNG MASTER TEACHER,
UNABLE TO GET TOP APPOINTMENTS, AN ORPHANED CHILD, WITHOUT REPUTATION
EXCEPT FOR DISCIPLES (MENCIUS COMMENTARIES, THE GREAT DIGEST
AND UNWOBBLING PIVOT (EP)) REVIVED IN 12TH
CENTURY AS OFFICIAL DOCTRINE FOR
CIVIL SERVANTS, WHO SAID
NOTHING ABOUT
GODS OR THE AFTERLIFE, JUST
TREAT 'EM RIGHT, DAMMIT, AND THEY'LL
BEHAVE AND BE HAPPY   GUANINE sudden end to breath
as the mind splashes briefly in heavy waters before settling
down and accepting the cold darkness / MERCURIC, I.E. TRANSFORMED
AND THE EARTH A CRUST OF SILICATES MINGLED WITH HYDROCARBONS CALLED
SOIL WHEN YOU MULCH ENOUGH DEAD LEAVES INTO IT, THE ROOT
OF THE GRAPE VINE GRIPPING THE ROCKS AND LYRA
WITH VEGA LIKE A BRIGHT NAIL OVERHEAD
OVERWHELMING ON A CLEAR NIGHT
MILES FROM TOWN / birds
call to each other
at twilight, sensing winter /
IF YOU HATE SOMETHING IN THE MAN AHEAD
OF YOU, DO NOT DO IT TO THE MAN WHO FOLLOWS YOU.
FROM THIS ROOT AND THIS HARMONY HEAVEN AND EARTH ARE ESTABLISHED.
(SUCH WISDOM FLOWS LIKE TIDEWASH THROUGH GENERATIONS IN AND OUT OF FAVOR).

GAEA, OUR MOTHER. SEEN FROM THE MOON SHE IS BREATHTAKING, FRAGILE, WONDERFUL.
OXYGEN ATMOSPHERE COMPLIMENTS OF BLUE GREEN ALGAE, DELICATE CRUST
THAT CHANGES WITH SEASONS, BUT IRON TO THE CORE,
MANTELLED WITH VAN-ALLEN BELTS TO BUFFER
THE WINDS FROM THE SUN, SHE HOLDS
IN PROTECTIVE LAYERS OF
BLUE-GREEN AIR
OUR HERITAGE, HISTORY AND
HOPE FOR CONTINUANCE / *you do not*
study landscape, you absorb it by living there,
the Innuit *in kayak sniffing air around glacier, bushmen*
finding water in desert, people like caribou and migratory waterfowl
covering the same route year after year without instruments beyond the imprint
of starpattern, rockpattern, horizon, deep pull of the floodplain
shaped on remembrance   GUANINE one green bush inflamed,
the cloud shaped like a horse, branches swish
and swash like sky brooms, bits drift
spindling to grass, fragments
from 10,000 years,
the dead float in midair, Saint
Matthew Passion and the slaughter at Hastings
of my namesake / *SULEIMAN, KANUNI (LAWGIVER) SURELY THE*
MOST CIVILIZED LORD OF HIS AGE (THOUGH HE STRANGLED HIS SONS)
INVADED REGULARLY THE SOFT UNDERBELLY, PUSHING TO WEIN, KILLING MAGYARS
WHILE THE REST OF THE CONTINENT WRESTLED OVER ROME, THE FRENCH FINALLY PURCHASING
THEIR POPE FOR A CENTURY, MORALS DECAYING WORSE THAN IN OUR OWN TIME,
SODOMY, ADULTERY, FORNICATION WITH ANIMALS COMMON, ALL RULES
ABANDONED IN EUROPE (EXCEPT IN THE CLOISTERS)
WHENCE COMETH BUBOES IN ARMPIT/GROIN
GRIM REAPING OF 25 MILLION /
windows of the soul
thrown wide every morning--ah!
history rich in the air, history of leaves
their tips curled up, dried out by industrial fumes,
clouds move inside my body as I lie sprawled on the grass littered

with leaves between clean-edged stones whose carved names blurr out of focus
T.J. AND V.N. AND JESSIE SHINDURLING children gone now and who
will remember which patterns I belong to, which changing
cloudbanks / DISCOVERED THE SUN MOST PROBABLY IS
NOT CENTRAL TO OUR UNIVERSE, FLOATED
THROUGH MILKY STARS IN HIS
18" REFLECTING TUBE
BILL HERSCHEL CATALOGUING THE COSMOS
FOR FUTURE TRAVELLERS / *Strabo began it (1 A.D.)*
this obsessive charting onto paper/papyrus/vellum instead of
sharpening senses/intellect (so that any damn fool can figure it out,
like navigating downtown Louisville after dark) and Vasco Da Gama tiptoeing
around the Cape w/o falling off (1498) so that every English/Spanish SOB
could hoist sail and name continents after himself, his King,
Queen, mistress or bastard (even his mapmaker) w/o
consulting the locals / DÜRER'S GOLDEN HAIR
AND GIBBETS OF BOSCH, DEMONS OUT OF
BELLY OF HUGE FISH,
COMETH CALVIN IN HIS BLACK CAP,
LUTHER NAILING TETZEL TO THE CHURCH DOOR
AND ALL THOSE MELANCHOLY PROTESTANTS REFORMING THE
GOSPELS (WYCLIF, ZWINGLI, HUSS) BY THE LIGHT OF BURNING MARTYRS
WHILE ENGLISH AND FRENCH SLAUGHTERED EACH OTHER AT CRECY / in the body
chemical libraries containing our history back to the blue-green algae, patterns
of instinct, landscape, fear/trembling, voice, drum, reed flute,
warcry and deathwail, lullabye beneath stars, tunk tunk katunk
of skin drum, buffalo and the deer / THIRD PLANET
MOST SUITABLE ALL ELEMENTS IN BALANCE AS IF
CREATED THAT WAY WHICH WE, BLIND
AS OEDIPUS, ARE RAPING
WITHOUT AWARENESS OF THE ENORMITY,
OUR OWN MOTHER DRAGGED TO THE WHOREHOUSE,
THE OZONE LAYER BURNED OFF, THE OCEANS/RIVERS POISONED,
FORESTS RAVAGED OF TIMBER, SOILS LEACHED OF NUTRIENT, EVEN THE RAIN
BURNS HOLES IN HER FACE, TIRESIAS A VOICE TO BE LAUGHED AT AND IGNORED,
THERE'S PLENTY MORE WHERE YOU CAME FROM BITCH / *Richard Hakluyt, Man of God,*

explores *the icy wastes & lives to write about it, Alexander von*
Humboldt tramping through the forest primeval trapped
the subject and tied it to the University /
HUNDREDS WOULD GATHER FOR A PUBLIC
HANGING OR TO SEE SOME POOR
BASTARD TORN TO BITS
BY A CHAINED BEAR, DAILY ENTERTAINMENTS
OUTSIDE (AND INSIDE) THE CATHEDERAL, BOCCACIO
AND GEOFFREY CHAUCER VENDYING HIS PILGRIMAGE OF PORTRAITS:
HUMANITY IN EXTREMIS / sing, O sing and cover yourself
with paint, with leaves, disguises, masquing changes, beat the skin
drum for a few hours, whistle the flute to yourself, life is transitory forever
changing, transforming, clouds behind trees, leaves falling like
children, like hours from the day, the mosque at
Astrakahn hovering like a dream over blue
water, sun behind clouds, chill
touching the body.

26.

ADENINE
Now Death enters
the air and takes possession.
Light frost on grassblades early morning,
leaves dropping like decayed teeth out of the trees /
Acetylsalicylic Acid by-product of coal-tar Charles Gerhardt 1853,
gathering foxglove, belladonna, crushing berries in pestle, such ancient alchemy
behind all pharmacy, rhino horn (they hunt them to extinction) with
aphrodisiac qualities, eye of newt, hair of bat, etc. . ./
Ditch water swirled brown as tea, sparkles
with golden highlights as the sun
bends through, crunch
of bootheels
breaking through ice
in the tiretracks of mud lanes,
how we are tied together, no one happy alone

but yearns for companions, parents, children, wife, workmate
losing them all eventually, bringing them here / "dark matter" from
the Big Bang, massless, affected by weak force and gravity only, blown off by
solar wind and the explosion of new stars, they migrate the curved
boundaries of infinite space penetrating with ease allthings
including ourselves / *BABY KUMP 1924* the dry flowers
commemorating faces we strain to remember
under the treelimbs kicking up
wet yellow leaves /
physical engineering you might
call it, this extending of life by cleverness,
barber/surgeons letting blood with a razor, leading to
artificial heart/lungs/valves/bloodvessels and Dr. Timothy Leary
having his head removed (after death) to be frozen and saved for future
Frankenstein resurrection, how far can we push immortality? / ah, hell--you know
what I'm talking about--Homer with his bright ships and helmeted gods,
Shakespeare, the old man howling on a precipice--what good
all this howling, these dreams of deathless heroes,
yellow leaves clinging to wet bootheels,
must still go home to dinner
read the newspaper,
tragedies unending, children
abandoned by parents, unprepared for life's
buffeting unfairness, who harden through defiant anger
into the lunatic spraying a restaurant with machinegun ultimate
wail of torn soul sucking thumb in a closet, Jesus, how can we allow it?
This is our living and dying, children--pay attention. / *I swear by Apollo,*
the physician, and Asclepius and Health and All-Heal, and all the
gods and goddesses that, according to my ability and
judgement, I will keep this oath / electromagnetic
force between two electrons is 10^{42}
times stronger than gravity
Thomson/Rutherford
carries negative charge opposed
to positron you can see the Cerenkov radiation
at night, gamma rays exciting the upper atmosphere causing

57

electron showers / *I will give no deadly medicine to anyone if*
asked, nor suggest any such counsel / After Labor Day darkness seems to
drop like a curtain around us, the Bear pivots on Polaris, Virgin descending,
and so many stars whose names I have not learned, Böotes the great
herdsman, Hercules and the square of Pegasus pulling
us into horizons binding us all, hunter and
herdsman, learned and ignorant, into
our memories, father bent over
fire, child in ashes,
mother offering breasts without
a second thought, lifegiver / *I will not*
give to a woman an instrument to produce an abortion.
I will not cut a person who is suffering from a stone, will
abstain from every voluntary act of mischief and corruption and further
from the seduction of females or males, bond or free / o my children (my own
children--you, Jennifer and Jonathan) be brave, do not lose heart,
there is infinite wonder and sorrow in living connected
to each other, follow the pattern, yield to
the pull of the earth and moon,
find lovers, engender
your own kind
and walk here long after
mother and I are memories carved into
flat stones the grass grows over, this is why
we are born, how we participate fully in human bondage
to earth and to each other, faithfulness more precious in long run
than any aberant desire, someone to trust utterly, to lie beside in the morning
as your mother and I hold each other tenderly at first light under
blankets warmed by our bodies all night, such happiness
is yours if you seek it over the long years,
seek it, my children, there is no
other reality, no other
immortality.

27.

Fragmentation . . .
floods, endless revolutions in
small nations, the collapse of major industrial powers,
shootings and executions, bullet behind ear, body pitching headlong
into mass grave, bayonet leaned on with full weight, clockwork
wound too tight, the terrible headlines fall on our heads daily
as we sit in our easy chairs after dinner covered with leaves / BUT THE MOON
NEVER CHANGES (BECAUSE SHE IS ALWAYS CHANGING) PULLING US OFF-BALANCE
AT BARYCENTER, WOBBLING IN ORBIT, SHE HAS SEEN IT ALL BEFORE /
wings moving up and down gently, black lined
with irridescent gold and crimson,
blue "eyes" this creature
alive for a few days /
PERMIAN, LAST PALEOZOIC PERIOD,
VIOLENT CRUNCHING OF CONTINENTS SHOVING UP
GREAT MOUNTAINS, ICE STRETCHING OVER AUSTRALIA, AFRICA
AND THE SEAS DRYING UP, LAYING THE GREAT SALT DEPOSITS / when we left,

it was raining. I woke in the night to see my naked foot silvered
with moonlight. Father's hands smelled of creosote. Falling off the tower
with no one to catch me. When we returned, my hair smelled like
     wet leaves / ROTATION 27.3 DAYS, GRAVITY ONE-SIXTH,
          AND TEMPERATURE SWINGS 300° C EVERY DAY /
               MANY SPECIES DIED, FIRST TREES
                    AND FERNS GIVING WAY TO
                         CONIFERS / CYTOSINE
               Grandfather's wingtips beside
          the clothestree, cane in the umbrellastand,
     feared deep water, looking down into it, bottomless,
watercolor done in childhood still hangs in her bedroom, Oh! to
run away! away! away! *PIO URRUCHUA, 1894-1952* / TRILOBITE
FINALLY EXTINCT, THOUGH REPTILES ADAPTED AND INSECTS AS WE
KNOW AND LOVE THEM FIRST APPEARED / Let me die
     young, I prayed each night / CRATERS
          ON BOTH SIDES NOW NAMED FOR
               EVERYONE UNDER THE SUN,
                    WE HAVE WEIGHED
                    AND MEASURED YOU,
                    O HUNTRESS, HAVE STEPPED
               ON YOUR FACE, KNOWING NONE OF
          YOUR SECRETS / Ashes and smoke. Ashes
     and smoke. Dragonflies hover and zoom on blurred wings.
The spruce with sunlight fully on it, the white marble mausoleum.
I am aware of the distance separating allthings, binding them
     at barycenter as we wobble in orbit together. Red berries
          pucker with frost, and tiny flakes, yellow and brown,
               drop at random in the smoky air.

                              28.

               THE UNCARVED BLOCK, OLD
                    MAN RIDING A WATERBUFFALO INTO
                         THE UNEXPLORED REGIONS / tump-tump, tump-tump
                    fife and drum, rosewood recorder, beaten sticks to bring

the old man dancing in, dried flowers knotted in
his hair, old man in a black coat, holloweyed,
dancing on dead leaves, in yellow grass, caught
in his own music. Totentanz / AND LEONARDO IN MIDLIFE
DESIGNING MACHINE GUNS FOR THE BORGIAS BETWEEN PAINTINGS / the Dipper
dips into the horizon, pulling up darkness / WHEN KUNG CAME VISITING
HE SAID: RID YOURSELF OF ARROGANCE, LUSTFULNESS AND YOUR
INGRATIATING MANNERS AND EXCESSIVE AMBITION. THEY
ARE ALL DETRIMENTAL TO YOUR PERSON / the polished fruit
of the chestnut tree bouncing from split husks
and ivy arching a crimson cape over
the dilapidated fence / THYMINE
THE WAY THAT CAN BE DESCRIBED OR NAMED
IS NOT THE WAY / AWAKENING SPIRITS, THE GREAT LORDS
OF CITY STATES SLAUGHTERING EACH OTHER WITH BLESSING OR CONNIVANCE
OF ONE POPE OR ANOTHER, JULIUS, LEO, CLEMENT, PRINCES OF POWER.
AND MACHIAVELLI TORTURED WITH FOUR TURNS OF THE RACK FOR DESERTING FLORENCE,
RETIRED AT SAN CASCIANO TO WRITE HIS REVENGE / the children and I
roll in the dry leaves and throw them into the air, singing
and dancing, scarecrow, leaves stuffed in my shirt,
lumbering over the stones. Totentanz /
IT IS THE WAY OF HEAVEN TO SHOW
NO FAVORITISM. IT IS
FOREVER ON THE SIDE OF THE GOOD MAN.
TURNING BACK IS HOW THE WAY MOVES. WEAKNESS
IS THE MEANS THE WAY EMPLOYS / maple leaves yellow and red
with waxy supple texture between fingertips, luxurious
over the humped graves of rich and poor, anglo and chicano, covering
the small stones of MARY ANSELMO and JOHN CEDERBERG like a democratic blanket
and it is privilege and miracle to be alive among the dead,
sucking in crystalline air, the body participating
without needing to philosophize, without
thought or the weight of tasks,
dancing, dancing / PAINTED THE SISTINE
AGAINST HIS WILL, ALL THE TIME MUTTERING
"THIS IS NOT MY TRADE!" WHO LOVED TO CARVE STONE,

FINDING HIDDEN WITHIN THE LIVING GRAIN CREATURES
CALLING FOR RELEASE, THE MOTHER OF GOD PONDERING HER PASSION
LAID ONCE MORE ON HER LAP, DAVID LOOKING OVER HIS SHOULDER
TOWARD PRAXITELES, THE SOUL AT PEACE ONLY WHEN WORKING IN SOLITUDE,
EXPLORING ETERNITIES OF FORM, ST. PETER'S DOME AND THE REST OF IT
CULLED FROM THAT DARK WRESTLING / once felt, it cannot be
forgotten. Unforgotten, it cannot be killed.
Unkilled, it continues, this
immortal delight, this dancing . . .
October thoughts, Dylan,
remembering your hilltop vision.
"and death shall have no dominion."
Totentanz. / HE WHO IS HERE IS RAPHAEL /
AND THE OLD MAN RODE OFF INTO THE SUNSET, AS IT WERE,
ON HIS BUFFALO, LOOKING BACK WITH ENIGMATIC SMILE: WHEN THE
PEOPLE LACK A PROPER SENSE OF AWE, THEN SOME AWFUL VISITATION WILL
DESCEND UPON THEM. LAO TZU. FIVE HUNDRED YEARS OR SO BEFORE CHRIST.
THE REASON I HAVE GREAT TROUBLE IS THAT I HAVE A BODY. WHEN I
NO LONGER HAVE A BODY, WHAT TROUBLE HAVE I? KNOW THE
MALE, BUT KEEP TO THE ROLE OF THE FEMALE.
ONE WHO EXCEEDS IN TRAVELLING
LEAVES NO WHEELTRACKS.

29.

Totentanz. Allthings
die. This fact of the stiff, dead thing
has to be dealt with.   It seems so easy, to become
dead. Dead bird, dead cat, insects stomped underfoot, and this
once-breathing human being now dead weight with oxygen tubes
in nostrils and air rushing out of the open mouth, those still-living
stand powerlessly by as the object is transformed, no longer human, a
mere dead thing, husk, to be dealt with by some professional wearing
plastic gloves in a room with antiseptic tiles, as we,
with our rituals of grief, move away, following
the flow of our lives / *origin of stones*

Theophrastus, 300 B.C. and Pliny
(the Elder) going out with Vesuvius.
Avicenna explained fossils as pre-born
plants and animals (1020), we are drawn to stone
in riverbank, broken from cliffwall, useful, first tool
and history book (if you can pry the pages apart) containing
all of our ancestors like leaves pressed between leaves of the World Book.
In the face of geological time, of what possible significance could be
this thin layer of days and years soiled with the campfires
of human life? / manipulation of others, driving to
consensus, balancing gains with trade-offs,
establishing rules / I found the kitten dying
of distemper in the drainage ditch,
killed it quickly with a
4x4 post and buried the body in a
garbage bag half-hour before the children woke up.
Am ! different in doing this without hesitation
from Eichmann, from IRA terrorists, from the Israelite Army
slaughtering men, women, children and livestock under direct orders
from Yaweh upon pain of death, scorched earth in the promised land,
or the man-made BIG BANG over Hiroshima/Nagasaki vaporizing
men/women/boys/girls/goldfish/birds/bugs/trees/grass
because IT HAD TO BE DONE and we had the
technology? / *Hammurabi 1700 B.C.*
established the code for
crime & punishment
equality before the law,
upon the heels of which come
ten thousand lawyers to make ten thousand   `
regulations from the Ten Commandments, indigestible
Digest of Justinian, Solomon's famous trial by dissection
and unending bickering of scribes over loopholes but it's better
than anarchy / Agassiz measuring glaciers projecting
iceages, evidence clear and not circumstantial
though we believe what we want to /
UNKNOWN INDIAN WOMAN 1957
but the earth knows her name

a mother knows
her child, no matter how lost,
named not by tongue or ridicule but in the
elements, in bone and blood, protein, cellulose as it
loosens, dissolves, re-enters the larger reality, the chemical
eternity of atoms exchanging energy levels, alchemy of what we term
death which is transformation one life to another / CYTOSINE
the everlasting hills of Utah were oceanbottom in the
Permian, seabed sediments tilted on end now
as the Wasatch fault lifts leviathan
from seafloor to skyfloor /
fragments, bone chips, attentionspan
cut to three seconds,
changing the channels constantly,
the mind leapfrogging context to context,
avoiding commercial messages, old sit coms, evangelists
and anything in the least stressful, pinball bouncing
from sensation to sensation, chipping the block
into ten thousand fragments, leaves, moments
scarce remembered, frozen in stone / *without order*
there can be no accomplishment, stone
cities, fields of grain, life
crossing generations;
without order
anarchy brings destruction
tearing the veil asunder
as we "bomb them back to the stoneage"
(Gen LeMay) in the name of survival /
read the rocks, it's all there
eons compressed to inches, the Grand Canyon
laid out like a rainbowed testament of time cataloguing all
mysteries, wordless, book of the dead /
while all we know for certain
is that we are ALIVE and belong to the living
and the dead belong to the earth,
to rocks and stars.

30

My son and I
walk after dinner. He has
a stick for rifle. We play at combat
among the stones, trees all heavy with gold /
HUNGARIAN REVOLUTION 1956, YOM KIPPUR WAR AND
CHARGE OF THE LIGHT BRIGADE / the sky soaks up darkness
and I fall down dead and look up into black branches.
I love my son more than anything / THYMINE
two million nephrons filtering
fifty gallons daily / he is hiding.
I count to one hundred
and roll off running from
stone to stone
pretending combat yet caught
by the exquisite maple half-empty of
orange leaves--and I realize: he is nowhere /
LIBRA HOLDS US IN BALANCE, VENUS
BRIGHTEST THIS MONTH WHEN DYLAN, ERASMUS
AND ST. FRANCIS ARE BORN / step out into the open expecting
sudden ambush. Nothing. Twinge of apprehension.
I call his name. No answer. Run back
through the rows of graves--
did he fall? Is he hurt somewhere?--
Has he been stolen away? /
DONALD FRUGOLI 1922
Reins the purifiers, Henle's
loop, Bowman's capsule and glomerulus
controlling the blood with erythropoietin /
Heartrate up now, running in full panic.
God he is so small. Where has he got to in this darkness.
God that he be not taken away from me! / AIR PUNGENT WITH SMOKE
FROM WOODSTOVES, ASPEN AND CEDAR, PUMPKINS
HEAVY YELLOW ALONG FENCELINE, APPLES
READY TO HARVEST, HUNTING SEASON

AND STARS OF AUTUMN RISING /
This place of trees and stones foreboding
in its gloaming hour, full of
hidden places. I laugh to myself
and my laughter is terrible. Where is he? /
Largest glandular organ quarterlobed,
hepatic duct carrying bile to bladder
and urea from proteins to kidneys for excretion /
Jon! I cry--Game's over!--Come out wherever you are!
Stand desperate in stillness, the twilight
filling dark space with smothering beauty.
O Death keep your hands off my boy.
I won't let you--you cannot
take him from me /
ALDEBARAN, AND THE PLEIADES
BRINGING UP ORION OVER THE DRY FIELDS,
ST. CRISPIN'S DAY AND AT THE END ALL
HALLOW'S EVE / Totentanz / regenerates itself
and manufactures glycogen for quick energy, also Vitamin A,
D, B_{12} and Iron / Then suddenly I see him
at the end of the lane, by the gate,
waiting for me. Ah, Jesus.
Jesus. Walk up as if nothing
were unusual and run my hand
through his hair, rumple his shoulder
and give him a hard hug.
Didn't you hear me? Yes.
Were you trying to scare me?
Yes. Dear God--how little it takes
to defeat me. A grown man in tears for a son
who was lost and has been given back. I know the power
that lies on every side. I know you could have kept him
if you wished. Dark trees, chill stones.
Thank you for giving him
back to me!

66

31

Wandered into middle Europe
            300,000 B.C. at Swanscombe,
        Steinheim, Homo Sapiens the stone-chipper /
        It rains today, cold, ashen rain
    of early winter. The chestnut tree stands naked,
    new leaves pressed into asphalt by car tires.
Will you take one home? A fresh one like a limpid flame
to be pressed in a dictionary while all its fellows are
    ground into fragments: à movie star made
        artificially immortal to represent
        "the best" of a season / *MYRNA LOY WEBB 1941*
            Acheulian tools of flint and quartzite
                struck off the core with a bone
                    hammer, this craft of
                millennia, honed to perfection
        and nothing more needed until agriculture
        brought warfare, lust for metals
    to protect property / TAU PARTICLE WITH ITS
CORRESPONDING NEUTRINO MORE MASSIVE THAN ELECTRON BUT
FUNCTION UNKNOWN / green leaf on black stone,
    Vivaldi's FOUR SEASONS, fragments falling nameless
        in grand democracy one on the other, like Jews in a
            mass grave outside Warsaw or the Indians at Sand Creek.
                Remember the names of the peoples who
                    got in the way: Micmac, Abenaki,
                Passamquoddy, Algonquin, Cherokee, Creek and
            Chikasaw, Osage, Choctaw, Comanche, Dakota and Mandan,
        Navajo, Hopi, Shoshone, Kiowa, Arapaho, Quapaw, Wichita, Zuni,
    Flathead, Blackfoot, Cheyenne, Chippewa, Potawatomi, Natchez, Seminole,
Lakota Sioux, Haida . . . and we gave them syphillis, whiskey and blankets with
    smallpox, paper treaties, gestures of peace / ADENINE
        crossed over Gibralter, driven by
        icecaps and bitter cold
            following bison, the magnificent

creature painted on cavewall,
hunting societies like wolfpacks
reverencing lifegiving beasts,
keeping the embers safe in a clay cup,
theirs the deep memories
patterned in our blood, the old fears
of cold and dark and terrible sabretoothed death /
TRACES VISIBLE ONLY IN CLOUDCHAMBER, INTRICATE
TIGHT SPIRALS DRAWN AT LIGHTSPEED /
Why do we kill one another?
Tell me, brothers and sisters.
We must look into ourselves.
Why this thick piling down of the dead
murdered by others?
We must look into ourselves,
Brothers and sisters.
Why do we kill one another?

32.

NAMED FOR PERCIVAL LOWELL WHO
DREAMED AFTER IT, THIS "PLANET X" BY
CLYDE TOMBAUGH PROVEN (1930) WITH ITS MYSTERY PARTNER
WALZING 248 YEARS AT 4.7 KM/SEC IN THE -230°
ICY DARKNESS, LORD OF THE SEASON /
and Mother born on All Saint's Day,
the Great Square of Pegasus high in the Southwest,
Andromeda (M31) 2 million light years away
Hercules marching over the rooftops . . .
A study in egg-tempera,
Wyeth's season, muddy leaves
and broken ice in the lane,
discarded tires, beer cans in the weed-choked ditch,
seeds and burrs catching jacket sleeves;
I sit on the cement bench, resigned to the drift of things /
MUON, MYSTERIOUS LEPTON, ZIPPING BY /

THIS MONTH, MARTINUS LUTHER, THE LITTLE MONK,
THIS MONTH HERR HITLER STRIDES UP LUDWIGSTRASSE,
THIS MONTH POPE URBAN II AND THE
FIRST CRUSADE, FIRST JUKEBOX
IN SAN FRANCISCO (1889)
AND LINCOLN DEACHEY'S FIRST LOOP-
THE-LOOP, SCORPIO DOMINANT, THE LEONIDS
RESPLENDENT AFTER MIDNIGHT, YOUTH DAY
IN THE UPPER VOLTA AND BARBED WIRE INVENTED, 1873.
PRUNE YOUR GRAVEVINES. GATHER FIREWOOD / Comes then a general
deterioration on all sides: teeth falling out, hair long gone, eyes
needing glasses to see across the street, empires weak
in the knees, barbarians rushing in with
waraxes whirling: Mongols, Huns,
Tartars, Visigoths, Vandals, whatever.
And no one remembers how the
aqueduct functioned
or cares to repair a broken arch.
Old masks are replaced with new.
Comes now bad weather, sleetstorms, blizzards,
broken statues, burned books, breakdown / and
two shin bones, a few teeth, original wise guy
one hundred thousand years before television and space flight
created scrapers, borers, burins, polyhedrals &
gravette points by hammering the core with
legbone socket, craftsman, all our
technology contained within
his dreaming / GUANINE
I give this day
to you. There are not many
like it, my son, my daughter, kicking
through dry leaves. I am 29, you are 9 & 6.
Life goes on forever, don't you think?
DONALD RADEMACHER 1923-1931 / COMPATIBLE WITH
PISCES, CANCER, PASSIONATE, INTENSE, SECRETIVE, SUBTLE,
OCCUPATION: TEACHING / Let's laugh and play and

roll in the leaves. See how the sun cuts through
the smoky air! / ZIPS BY LIKE A BLUE
DRAGONFLY, ONE SECOND OF ONE
DAY IN YOUR LIFE: MUON /
Let's run!

33.

Conserving energy, always
a transformation to heat, light or
sound, vibrant, at the core of atomic structure
photons exchanging / Do not think that people are simple.
We carry complexities, each of us, even the least talented, holy,
unknowable. We only appear to be ordinary / *Faraday & Maxwell,*
electromagnetic waves, radio/television in embryo /
SIDDHARTHA GAUTAMA IN THAT ELECTRIFYING FIFTH
CENTURY ABANDONS WIFE AND INFANT SON
TO SIT BENEATH BODHI TREE / I say
to really look into the eye of another
is to see eternity / THREE
REFUGES, THREE JEWELS, TRIPTKA /
Each face an angel. Each eye
a universe. Leaf upon leaf. Stones in a pile.
Soul in a pool of souls. Light from the stars.
Do not esteem yourself to be small. You are
galactic. *EUNICE HUNT (HER HANDMADE STONE) 1931-1932* / ADENINE
THE CYCLE OF LIFE IS PAIN. ENLIGHTNEMENT IS KNOWING
RELEASE IN NON-ATTACHMENT. BODHISATTVA CHOOSES
SERVICE CVER NIRVANA / *Levers & liquids,*
but mathematics its language,
measuring speed of falling bodies,
movement through time,
the quanta most satisfying that can be
repeated perfectly anywhere / AVOID EXCESSIVE SATISFACTION
AND EXCESSIVE SELF-DENIAL / The first snow
falls today, flakes big as leaves, the sharp wind

70

cutting through my coat like a chainsaw / KNOW TRUTH, RESIST EVIL,
DO NO INJURY WITH WORDS, RESPECT LIFE, MORALITY, PROPERTY, DO NOT
    INJURE OTHERS IN YOUR WORK, FREE THE MIND OF EVIL, CONTROL
        THOUGHTS AND FEELINGS, PRACTICE CONCENTRATION / easy
            to say, but how many choose it? At forty
                I am beginning to learn how to make
                    love to my wife. Is it unwise
                        to risk attachment to another?
                    Suffering is also a good path
                up the mountain / *sum total of matter & energy*
        has not diminished in twenty billion years,
    only exchanged at all levels two million trillion times. ◆

                                34.

And for those of you who have already figured this out and are
bored with it, disappointed with the metaphor, hip to my cleverness in
    following what has been done before and better (I know it and
        there are no apologies) I wish you good roasting and
            toasting me on the spit of your wit--you also
                are part of the process / CHARLES MESSIER CATALOGUING
                    HIS 100 GALAXIES FROM THE ROOFTOPS OF PARIS
                        AND HUBBLE AT MT. WILSON MEASURING
                    RED SHIFT / *the desire to heal*
                less motivating perhaps than the desire to
            excel in this most difficult craft, scalpel and clamp,
        not even the pericardial cavity sacrosanct / GUANINE
and you who do not understand it at all and have quit reading
long ago in discouragement, come back again in a few years, don't be
concerned about all the detail--it's only names and dates--
    what you find in any cemetery or history book--
        don't take it too seriously / between
            the legs for protection as
                well as convenience the
                    penis and vagina
                wait for each other's call /

                                71

AND FARTHER AWAY THE FASTER THEY FLY, 3C295
SHOOTING OFF AT ONE THIRD LIGHT SPEED PROVING THE
BIG BANG / Wrote the first draft in a notebook back in 1975
hoping at that time to recreate SONG OF MYSELF. Ten years afterward
started the first serious rewrite, put it away, knowing I wasn't ready
and may not yet be ready for the poem even now, though the time
is right and there is no turning back now that we've come
this far / *Crawford Long the first to use ether,*
Joseph Lister spraying the room down with
carbolic acid, and now they lift
the heart out in both hands
like Peruvian priests at the altar /
egg only lives for twelve hours and the
sperm like a salmon surging upstream to plant
itself headfirst in the promised land / Ezra
and Eliot and Bill Williams also examples, though this can't hold
a candle to THE CANTOS, WASTELAND, ASPHODEL and the rest of it,
still I followed your boot-tracks far as I could before
cutting off into the trees on this unmarked trail
to end up where I've been headed from the
start / *PIERRE & PHILOMENE SERVEL* / LIGHT OLDER
THAN OUR KNOWLEDGE OF TIME JUST ARRIVING
FROM CORONA BOREALIS / *Colostomy,*
Mastectomy, Prostactomy, Splenectomy, Appendectomy,
Hysterectomy / labia, vulva, seminal
vesicle, testicle, scrotum, fallopian, oviduct,
where it comes from & goes makes a vas
deferens / and in back of it all, this beautiful english garden
of the dead, where I have found comfort and solace for sixteen years
and where they have almost fenced out the living and are in
the process of cutting down the magnificent trees each
year another one gone, the elms dying, dammit
in that lane where each time I walk I remember my
mother because she would have loved the
beauty of it in autumn with
its obvious poetry scattered everywhere,

yet the HUMAN BEING affirms by vigorous kicking of
leaves high in the sky that I AM STILL ALIVE IN THE WORLD
with fingers spread to feel air moving between them and nostrils
flared to suck in coldness exhaling steam, I REJOICE! that my name does
not mark one of these stones, though I know it is only a matter of time
and have made peace with all that--or am trying to do so here--
as she did, who is sixteen years into the mystery,
her father, Walther Schmidt, the only man
who could smoke cigars in her house
gone this very day also, a song for him
as he enters the stream / you with your
46 chromosomes, me with mine,
mixing our bloodlines with semen,
from which union one girl, one boy with
your eyes, my chin, your nose, my stubborness
as we become visibly one flesh to live beyond ourselves
as during the act we are mythic for a moment, you the
ur-mother, gaea, goddess, dark and libidinous,
I, priapus, the ramrod plunging, who in
this private darkness ever desires
another lover is a **god-damned**
fool darling because one
flesh is all flesh.

35.

AND THE PRIESTS WERE SO IMMORAL THAT
THE SYNOD OF 386 COMMANDED CELIBACY AS A
LAST DITCH STOP-GAP THOUGH EVEN A DIRECT ORDER FROM
THE POPE COULDN'T STOP THE HOUSEKEEPER MISTRESSES, SEDUCTIONS
IN THE CONFESSIONAL AND AUGUSTINE PRAYING "GIVE ME CHASTITY, LORD, BUT
NOT YET!" MEANTIME CONSTANTINE FOUNDED THE "NEW ROME" ON THE BOSPORUS
MAY 11, 330 A.D. / snowfall at night, without warning, caps
the corpses of sunflowers bending in crisp prayer,
laying a perfect inch on treelimbs untouched
by wind, air blue-brilliant before

sunrise, each stone chiseled by
cold, made taciturn, magnificent /
MESOZOIC, 230 MILLION YEARS AGO, TRIASSIC TIME
OF THE ARTHROPOD, CROCODILE & LIZARD DOMINANT LIFEFORMS /
EACH YEAR THE VISIGOTHS GOT BOLDER, ALARIC SACKING
THE CITY AT LAST IN 410, GAESERIC HAULING AWAY GOLD
INCLUDING TREASURES FROM SOLOMON'S TEMPLE THAT WAS
RANSACKED BY TITUS, AND ATTILA (LITTLE FATHER) BEFORE HE CHOKED ON HIS
OWN BLOOD (VESSEL BURST IN BRAIN WHILE SPORTING IN BED),
WITHDREW FROM CATALUNIAN FIELDS LEAVING 162,000 CORPSES,
AND IN 476 ODOACER TOOK CHARGE AND THAT WAS
THE END OF IT / the old man CYTOSINE
released from heaviness into
harmonious crystalline music,
snowflakes in midair, harpsichord preludes
and fugues of glass, November 11, 1975,
veteran of seventy-two years, he passed
into pure light, my grandfather / MOHAMMED ON BURAQ
FLYING AROUND JERUSALEM IN HIS VISION, AND HAD NOT
THE JEWS PISSED HIM OFF HE WOULD HAVE NAMED THAT HOLY CITY THE QIBLA
INSTEAD OF MECCA. ISLAM, FIRED BY DESERT VICTORIES WITH
THE QUR'AN FOR CONFIDENCE, SWEPT ACROSS AFRICA
THREATENING CHRISTENDOM, THE IDEA THAT
UNLEASHES ENERGY, A STRUCTURE FOR
LIVING AND DYING, EXQUISITE CRAFTSMEN
IN IVORY AND ENAMEL / joggers
undiscouraged by snowmelt trot through the trees,
one stopping to stare at a headstone, caught
by a name, and the new grave with its raw
heap of dirtclods and baskets of withered flowers
blanketed and beautiful this morning, where has he
gone that old skeptic, nazi industrialist, pianist,
what does he know? / AND AFTER FIVE HUNDRED DARK AGES
THEY RAISED STONE CATHEDERALS ALL OVER EUROPE / Sacrament of
ashes, farewell to the dead turned brown as flowers
on the dirtheap, music attend him forever /

74

ANGUS MCDONALD 1897-1924 / MAIMONIDES, SEPHARDIC
JEW IN MOORISH SPAIN, WRITING HIS GUIDE
TO THE PERPLEXED, AS WELL AS A TREATISE ON HEMORRHOIDS,
APHRODISIACS, AND THE MISHNA TORAH, ABELARD REFT OF HIS
MANHOOD AND THE INQUISITION, THAT LOVELY INVENTION,
TORTURING THOUSANDS OF BELIEVERS IN GOD'S NAME,
CRUSADERS SLAIN BY THE SWORD FOR THE GLORY OF
ALLAH (OR BRINGING HOME SPICES AND TRANSLATIONS OF ARISTOTLE)
WHILE IN TENOCHTITLAN THEY BUILT A MAGNIFICENT CITY
AND MAPPED OUT THE HEAVENS AND PLOTTED THE
UNIVERSE WITH NO THOUGHT OF THE
APPROACHING SPANIARD.

36.

PETER NUTT, 1950 /
protons last forever /
FIRST MAMMALS, FIRST BIRDS APPEAR /
BORN 100 B.C. OF AURELIA BY CUTTING THE BELLY /
sluice of snow like water blown over stone /
composed of 3 quarks by the strong force bound, positive
charge, with neutrons making up most of the mass of the
universe, waves on a string / PAID HANDSOME RANSOM TO CILICIAN PIRATES
RETURNING LATER TO CRUCIFY THEM / we give thanks
for wind-tight doors, food in pantry,
warmth & shelter, light &
friendship standing between us
and the cold blast / THYMINE
STEGOSAURUS, BRONTO-
SAURUS, ALLOSAURUS, TYRANNO-
SAURUS AND ALL THE SORRY THUNDERLIZARDS
SINKING INTO THE TARPITS AND COALFIELDS,
DIPLODOCUS 85 FEET LONG WITH A 2 OUNCE BRAIN,
PTERANODON & PTERODACTYL THE WILDEST EXPERIMENTS IN FLIGHT
AS IF GOD, LIKE LEONARDO, HAD TO WORK OUT HIS GRANDIOSE
IDEAS BEFORE CONCEDING THE MORE PRACTICAL BIRDS /

75

and that afternoon Jon fell off the sled
     and bloodied his lip on a stone hidden under snowbank;
        we packed his mouth with snow leaving
           small red stars on the whiteness
              as if an animal had been shot there /
                AH, CHRISTCHILD, BORN TO DIE,
                HOLLYBERRIES ON WHITE LEAVES
              PIERCE ME LIKE NAILS / in a salt mine in Ohio
     eight thousand tons of water wait for the decay of one
  proton proving entropy / chill wind in the body,
proving mortality, a day home with the flu,
     knotted, pierced with iron spikes in stomach & bowels,
        I know how it will be when darkness begins
           to inhabit this strung flesh /
              "OMNIUM MULIERUM VIR ET
                 OMNIUM VIRVORUM MULIER"
                    THAT WAS THE GOING JOKE
                 ABOUT THE BALD ADULTERER, BREAKING
              VERCINGETORIX AT ALESIA (52 B.C.) AFTER
           HIKING OVER THE ALPS IN WINTER, AND 300,000 HELVETII
        OUTFOXED AT BIBRACTE, ALWAYS ONE STEP AHEAD OF
     DISASTER SWIMMING THROUGH ARROWS WHILE THE LIBRARY AT ALEXANDRIA
BURNED IN THE NIGHT FROM THE SPARKS OF HIS GALLEYS, CALPURNIA
AWOKE SCREAMING FROM BLOODY DREAM AND HE: WHAT IS THE
     BEST DEATH? A SUDDEN ONE. 3-14-44 B.C. /
        The cancer came suddenly filling
           her belly like death's child and it was
              to late to do much but give her time to finish
                 university courses, graduate and die;
              the old man lasted longer of leukemia
           but it wore him out also, shrinking
        that tall, muscular master-sergeant
     into a dry leaf crippled in everything but spirit,
  and they were both glad to be out of it at last,
embracing death as a friend (see the print by
     Kollwitz) as one lost in a blizzard will lie down to sleep /

76

TENTMAKER FROM TARSUS, THIS PHARISEE OF PHARISEES
PERSECUTED THE LITTLE CHRISTS BEFORE HIS ENLISTMENT
ON ROAD TO DAMASCUS SMACKED BETWEEN THE
EYES WITH A 2X4, "WHO ARE YOU,
LORD?" / CLASSIC EXAMPLE
OF PENDULUM SWING, FREEDOM IN DESIGN,
TRYING OUT ALL VARIATIONS, AND WE MAKE FUN
OF THESE BIG-AS-BARN THUNDERLIZARDS BECAUSE THEY
GOT WIPED OUT (WE WHO HAVE NOT BEEN HERE FOR OUR FIRST
FIFTY MILLION YEARS) THE VOLCANIC JUNGLES STILL MORE
PEACEFUL FOR ALL THAT BELLOWING THAN OUR SO-CALLED
MODERN WORLD / It is pain that defeats us,
we cannot surmount except by submitting and letting it
carry us over the edge / ORGANIZED WHAT
BECAME THE UNIVERSAL, CATHOLIC,
HOLY AND APOSTOLIC CHURCH
BY POWER OF HIS INTELLECT NOT TO
MENTION DOGGED DETERMINATION
AND WILLINGNESS TO SUFFER,
THIS BALD, DEFORMED, UNPLEASANT
STORM-TROOPER FOR CHRIST
CROSSED INTO MACEDONIA RETRACING
ALEXANDER, FROM PHILLIPI TO ATHENS INTO CORRUPT
CORINTH RECONQUERING THE WORLD.

37.

Cogito, ergo sum . . .
or so he thought, geometric axioms
not always applying as cleanly to this world
with its messy emotions as to that pythagorean/euclidian
platonic universe of eternal forms, just
when you think you have it wired, here
comes Aristotle with his steeltape /
TIME OF THE ARCHER, OVERHEAD ORION
UNSHEATHS HIS SWORD IN EASTERN SKY, VISIBLE
EACH NIGHT AS I WALK THE DOG AROUND THE CHURCH CORNER,

THE PLEIDES LEADING TAURUS WITH ALDEBARAN AND HYADES, GEMINIDS
VISIBLE AFTER MOONSET NEEDLEPOINTING DARKNESS,
COMES SOLSTICE, NADIR OF LIGHT, MOST
SENSIBLE CRITTERS ASLEEP IN CAVE OR UNDER
ICE DEEP IN THE COLD MUD / the brief daylight
drawn into leafsmoke, no birds visible,
sallow cheeks, mouth agape, teeth
like shriveled seeds / *to first drive the nail*
and hang an entire structure from it, or to
build from the bottom up, from facts in hand
and what is known without doubt (if you can agree on it),
creating both ways a glass goblet filled with intellect
to spill on the next generation / stone molded from cement and formed
with a finger one afternoon in 1944, this infant, unforgotten
by parents now forgotten, half covered with leaves,
all things coming home in the earth / JOHN LENNON MURDERED
IN THIS MONTH, FIRST TRANSATLANTIC RADIO SIGNAL
AND BALLBEARING ROLLER SKATE PATENTED
1854, BORN NOW WALT DISNEY &
EMILY DICKINSON, KIT CARSON, PABLO
CASALS, OUTSIDE THE DAKOTA THE FORGETTABLE
EGOMANIAC WAITS WITH HIS REVOLVER / *Reality is allthings*
to all people, open for interpretation, a tough nut to crack:
Faith seeking understanding (Aquinas), Tabula Rasa (Locke),
"To Be is to be Perceived" (Berkeley), and the more we study mathematics,
applying cartesian logic and linguistic analysis the less
certain we are that anything can be known although
this doesn't prevent us from buying groceries
and making love to each other / we bring them here,
after life has broken them, the young mother
killing herself on the grave, friends
finally given up to heart attack or any of a thousand
fatal diseases, the long hospital seige ended,
victims of accident or violence, and the octogenarians
slipping away at peace in their beds, wife and husband
buried side by side, the children three sections down

78

as they fill the place up by decades, how do I
        love thee, let me bring thee flowers, or if I cannot
            (separated by 1,700 miles) let me lay flowers on the names I know
                after so many years, almost related to them, my people
                    and so much emotion unspoken in each stone /
                        BENJAMIN ACHIN 1871-1929 / CYTOSINE
                            perhaps the Sophists win out after all
                        Socrates, despite good questions,
                    even despite attempts to resurrect metaphysics
                in this age of Process & Reality, Ethics
            proceeds from those in power and all else
        is just bullshitting on the front porch after dark,
Meister Eckhart as close as anyone to the truth /
        KING OF GODS, ORBITING SUN EVERY ELEVEN YEARS AT PONDEROUS
            13KM/SEC, MOST BEAUTIFUL SWIRL OF CLOUDPAINT CRYSTALS
                OF AMMONIUM HYDROSULFIDE, THUNDERER, DRAGGING
                    AN ENTIRE COURT OF MOONS & ASTEROIDS
                        WHO HAD HOPED PERHAPS FOR A
                            RESURRECTED SUN, YOU
                        REMAIN UNKINDLED, COLD, MAJESTIC
                    CROWNED WITH YOUR THIN RING / The young couple
                walking from parked car to the small stone
            with a basket of flowers / *comes back to us*
        because it is ours to begin with,
I think, therefore . . .

                            38.

I think toward the stranger
    who will touch me after my death,
        you--whoever you are--whether you must pull me
            from wreckage unrecognizable or from some hospital bed,
                or perhaps (fortune permitting) from my own bed,
                    zipping me into a body-bag to haul to the morgue,
            I wish you no ill, have already forgiven
        whatever jokes you will make as you wash me up,
            dispose of my blood and my vital organs prior to cremation,

the function once done by family and friends now consigned to you,
professional stranger, priest of cadaver, innocuous mortician, member
perhaps of Kiwanis and Lions Club, taxpayer, ordinary joe
privileged to view my naked (and probably unsightly if not humorous)
remains--only this I ask: do not weigh, measure or try to
figure anything out--no autopsy please, unless
mandated by circumstance--the mystery
dissolved with me and is not
contained in the vehicle / ADENINE
LOCAL GROUP TWO MILLION LIGHT YEARS ACROSS
CONTAINS LARGE AND SMALL MAGELLANIC CLOUDS,
DRACO, ANDROMEDA, LEO I & II, NGC6822 AND SOME OTHERS--
STARS WITHOUT NUMBER / *Sigmund exploring the convolutions of dreams,*
the Id bound in a straight jacket of bourgeoise morality, ladies
who envied the penis, shoe clerks who lusted for mama, scribbled
notes in a notebook, artifacts brought up from the cavern
where the great smoking bison charges across
the limestone walls of the soul /
Totentanz. Blue smoke of evening,
snow lining the inner curve
of chiseled letters, no footsteps but mine,
greaved trunks of maples minutely decorated, the grainy
white marble lambs, plastic daffodils shiver in a mason jar and
tiny corners of ice in sombre numerals.
MERLIN JACK HALL, 1920 / UND HERR ALBERT EINSTEIN
SMOKING HIS PIPE IN THE PATENT OFFICE THINKING ABOUT CLOCKS /
Collective unconscious, the pattern deeper than blood, mandala,
god in us, with us, emerging in language, in stone,
and he built himself a tower late in life
and had particular love of totem objects,
the man in the pencil box, power
of the secret / SPACE
AND TIME NOT FIXED BUT RELATIVE
TO THE VIEWER, HIS SPEED AND SO FORTH,
MATTER AND ENERGY INTERCHANGEABLE, ALL THIS
BEFORE HE WAS 26 YEARS OLD / The first night out of the body.
Its first week under the grass. First month. First hundred years.

Grass comes and goes, grows, is cut, dies, and leaves emerge and fall down
    again and again, trees cut down, new ones planted, and still the
        mountains are there, some kind of sky, sunlight, clouds.
            And where will I be? / FASCINATED BY COMPASS NEEDLE AT AGE 5,
                "SOMETHING DEEPLY HIDDEN IS BEHIND THINGS."
                    WORKING OUT THE MATHEMATICS TOOK
                        THE REST OF HIS LIFE
                    AND STILL HE COULD NOT BEND THE NUMBERS
                TO FIT A UNIFIED FIELD THEORY, COULD NOT MATCH
            HIS SOCKS, CARED NOT A WHIT FOR FASHION,
        HATED NAZI'S, CHAMPIONED ZIONISTS (BUT WOULD NOT
    BE PRESIDENT OF ISRAEL) AND TOUCHED THE COSMIC CLOCKWORK
WITH HIS MIND, GONE INTO PIPESMOKE, HIS UNERASED BLACKBOARD LEFT AS A
    SHRINE TO HUMANITY, A HIGH WATER MARK / *for those requiring*
        empirical data we have mankind in a Skinnerbox
            pressing the right levers, responding to
                shock troops, lashes, verbal
                    and physical abuse, boot camp,
                        brainwashing and electric therapy
                    without much compassion, needle
                skittering on a chart, here is your problem,
            you are a goddamned human being, you poor bastard,
        differentiated from the white rat by your tears /
    Nor does it matter after death
what god you prayed to in what church
    or if you prayed at all to any god,
        prayer being a survival technique of the embodied soul
            necessary no longer. If there is another life
                who can avoid it? If there is nothing
                    but sleep, who will awaken?
                        We take what we are given (daily bread)
                    and when it's over, go where we are lead.
                The body is the only living church.
            Breathing is the only real prayer.
        And god by any name is either
    there or not there . . .

39

Serenity.
   Old grass in midwinter sunlight.
      Bark-torn branches shaped like human bones.
         Totentanz.   /

                       THYMINE
          Mousterian tools,
            La Ferrassie gravesites.

                           End of the third interglacial
                                flowering and they
        buried their dead turned sideways
           as if in sleep.
                      /   Adductor longus,
        gracilis, sartorius, rectus femoris,
        tensor fasciae, strength in
        lifting/running
                       /   hooves on stone, sandaled feet
     stirring up dust, helmeted eyes, shields, spear shafts
   between wall in phalanx, 6,000 years we have had
metal working, refining tools of war   /
                      THE SACRIFICIAL GOD
    JEHOVA IS SALVATION, TITLED "THE CHRIST"
     BY GREEKS, WHICH MEANS "ANNOINTED ONE"
      AS DOES "MESSIAH" IN HEBREW,
       KING DAVID'S HEIR, LAMB OF GOD,
        PRESAGED IN ISAIAH 53, PSALM 22,
         A MAN OF SORROWS, ACQUAINTED WITH GRIEF /
                           Totentanz /
        an de hipbone connected to de ilium,
       pubis connected to de iliacus,
      femur connected to da kneebone
                 (will these bones live?)
    now hear da woid ob da lard . . . /
              75,000 years ago
  all over Europe and across Siberia,

decorating bone spear-throwers and harpoon barbs,
    jewelry from bone, carved flute, hand-formed earth-mother
        with floppy breasts, huge belly and hips, and certainly language
            though no writing, no need, the long night stories
                remembered verbatim, taught by firelight
                                    /   Totentanz.
                Midwinter spring, he called it,
                    cycles colliding, crashing on seawall,
                though trees are not deceived
            by sunlight, sap remains in the root,
        bud lips still sealed against frost
    and the body--my body--stretches in cold brilliance
on a concrete bench, brushing off birddroppings
one week before Christmas, madiera swirled
    in the wineglass
                        /   GREATER LOVE HATH NO MAN . . .
    AND THE UNIVERSE PARTICIPATES IN THE METAPHOR,
        EXCHANGES OF ENERGY, PARENT DYING FOR THE CHILD,
            GENERATIONS OF CREATURES LIVING FOR THE NEXT GENERATION
            AND HE CALLED IT LOVE, MEANING THAT
                I CARE MORE ABOUT YOUR WELL-BEING AND FUTURE
                THAN MY OWN LIFE AND AMBITIONS
                                    /   *BABE OF HENRY*
        AND CORA FINGERLOS, 1921   /
                                    at the end of all ages,
        end of the world, the wars long over,
    this afternoon of still sunlight
    in the presence of the dead
at the end of all greeness
                        Serenity   /
                                    Neandertal.
    Most seem to have lived peacefully,
        accepting boundaries, cooperating on hunts,
            very few buried with wounds, and even the crippled
                cared for by tribe into mid-age
                            /   THE LORD, ADONAI

```
        WORD MADE FLESH, LOGOS
              CREATIVE RIGHT HAND OF THE FATHER
           "THIS IS MY BODY, MY BLOOD,
           TAKE AND EAT AND REMEMBER
         MY SACRIFICE"

                                    /

                              hard work, chiseling
         the new grave out of frozen clay, child
      of God and Man, I think of you
   coming in this coldness--and not all of it the weather--
      confronting our hardhearted sin like a chisel to break us down--
         out of compassion, because there is no other way
            to reveal your nature, the gift
              we do not deserve and hardly expected.
              Whistles to himself, jackhammering and
                  swinging the pickax overhead, working up a sweat.
                     Totentanz.

                               /          MOST RADICAL
             TEACHER OF RIGHTEOUSNESS
             BREAKER OF BARRIERS, PREACHING
           HOPE TO CAPTIVES, EQUALITY TO SLAVES
         AND WOMEN AND GENTILES AND THOSE OF NO STATUS
      TO THEM ESPECIALLY MERCIFUL, KIND, RECEPTIVE
   THIS LORD OF THE UNIVERSE, CARPENTER, RABBI, JESUS, MESSIAH, THE CHRIST
      LIFTED INTO THE HOT SUN, RAISED FROM THE COLD TOMB,
         UNEXPLAINABLE TO THIS DAY, THE SHROUD OF
            TURIN BAFFLING THE EXPERTS,
              DESPITE ALL THE MURDERS DONE IN HIS NAME, STILL
                 THE WAY OF SALVATION FOR A FEW, THESE
                    "LITTLE CHRISTS" AMONG WHOM
                 ST. FRANCES, MOTHER THERESA, ALBERT SCHWEITZER,
              DEITRICH BONHOFFER, SOULS POURED OUT ON THE ALTAR OF SACRIFICE
           COMPLETELY IRRATIONAL, NOT IN SELF-INTEREST, YET HAGGIOS,
         SEPARATED FROM THE REST OF US, HOLY, MOST HUMAN, GODLIKE
      CREATED IN HIS IMAGE, NAKED COMING AND GOING,
   BROKEN WAFER AND BLOOD ON THE STONE      /
```

                        Serenity.
THYMINE
                                          Totentanz.   /
     Carefully buried, knees pulled up, a stone
        placed over the head /
                                    In the fragments of ages,
           bone chips, flint chips, artifacts
              like fallen leaves and dry branches underfoot,
                 "Who are you, Lord?"
                                    /
                                          LORD
           OF THE DANCE
                       /
                 Totentanz.

40.

Memory is survival. Remember
  the Christchild, harmonizing
    the Universe like a
        rose curled in the
            imagination,
                bringing
            light and hope
        into the broken world.
        CASPAR EGGARTH, MELCHOIR
        AUERNIG, tonight I will be
your Balthazzar . . .

UNCERTAINTY
OF POSITION
TIMES UNCERTAINTY OF
VELOCITY TIMES MASS
CAN NEVER BE LESS THAN
PLANCK'S CONSTANT . . .

                              Discovered by James Chadwick,
                                Cambridge College, 1932
                                    three quarks, 2 up,
                                      one down . . .

                GUANINE
We are the Magi,
     seeking the Lord of Life
        in all His human forms . . .
                                              WERNER
                                           HEISENBERG,
                                        1926: THE MORE
                                    ACCURATELY YOU ATTEMPT TO
                                 MEASURE POSITION, THE LESS
                              ACCURATELY YOU CAN MEASURE VELOCITY
                              AND VICE VERSA--HENCE PARTICLES
                                 EXIST IN CLOUDS OF
                                    UNCERTAINTY . . .

             Let us lay a wreath
                on everyone . . .

                                       the unsexed other
                                            buffering
                                     between forces
                                  necessary for balance,
                              non-combatant best friend
                           bound to the center preserving
                    harmony, peace between particles . . .

          EINSTEIN COULD NEVER
        BUY INTO IT, "GOD
     DOES NOT PLAY DICE."
HEISENBERG: SO WHAT? . . .

                              Christmas morning around ten,
                                 I visit the Irish nuns--
                                    sun aflame in frosty air,
                                       Morning, Sisters!
                                          Bridegroom's
                                       born again! . . .

                              87

NEXT RING OUT, 75 MILLION
    LIGHT YEARS, THE LOCAL SUPERCLUSTER:
        VIRGO, URSA MAJOR, CANES VENATICI,
            M66, M96, M101, NGC5128, NGC1023,
                EACH A BILLION OR MORE STARS CAUGHT
                    IN SPIRALS AND DUSTCLOUDS . . .
                        GUANINE
                        Without memory we cannot recall
                         the way home, we touch the
                           hot stove twice, victims
                             of fierce competitors,
                               patterns printed
                                 chemically
                            in the gray matter
                        among them, faces and
                      voices, those we love, who
                  leave us to re-enter the earth
              yet are more real and present than
                the gas station attendant or
                  store clerk serving us
                      this moment . . .

        Neutron: mass
      but no charge . . .

                        sandstone so
                          weatherworn
                    like the mind at
                  95 years, all it says
             is: *PERPE   L M   RY OF . . .*

                41.

      Dordogne valley in Acquitaine,
    limestone plateaus, sheltering cavewall,
the people, clothed in skins, moccasins, hooded caps,
  working leather with their teeth to soften it,
     needles of ivory, bone flutes . . .

GUANINE

                              Now I see my father, his broad
                          back, brown leather jacket, hat with
                              the eartabs down, walking the
                                  dog among barren trees.
                                  He is smoking and
                                      the dog ranges
                                              here & there
                                      as dogs will do.
                                  Now my mother is also
                              walking with them . . .

       Rediscovery,
              sculpture unearthed by crusaders,
                 dark ages split open revealing older peoples,
           and pretty soon every Duke in Christendom was
         bringing home marble gods/goddesses to
       decorate his lawn, Pompeii discovered by farmers, 1748
   and Lord Elgin stripping the Parthenon circe 1812 . . .
                              Objects treasured for utility,
                          decorated, guarded, eventually buried
                              with the owner, shell, arrowpoint
                              or spearthrower, without
                                  these & a few bones
                                  we know nothing,
                                          no names,
                                  no faces . . .

& the flesh is spindrift, an obstacle.
       Spirit is all. Stephen Hawking in his wheelchair
           croaking out cosmic equations, Joni Eareckson
               painting with her teeth . . .
                                  While Boney's boys
                                were shooting the nose off
                              the Sphinx, Champollion dug the
                          Rosetta Stone, Paul Emile Botta
                            uncovered the palace of Sargon II,
                              May the King live forever . . .

89

Ice sheets reaching into Germany
covering most of England, sea level
dropping so that you could walk across
English Channel and Bering Strait,
the People with their dogs dragging sledges
following animals, wandering the planet.
This is the great Dreamtime spoken of,
harsh winter, survival requiring memory,
fire carried crosscountry, stopping places,
here the salmon always run, here
the musk ox and caribou . . .

Legal graverobbers,
Schliemann at
Troas and
Mycenae, Evans
digging up Knossos
and Lord Carnarvon/Carter
hauling out King Tut's treasure
safe for 3,000 years . . .

GUANINE
and not even memory
preserves the person, unknowable
(my strapping son, my lovely daughter born this day)
beneath the surface, just as my own mother could not know
the poetry of anger, lust and sorrow born in me
out of her flesh. Artifacts, what we leave behind,
this is all we have, along with stories,
lies, skewed remembrances, myths and a few letters . . .

The poor damned Neandertals
killed off suddenly
around 30,000 B.C.
uncompetitive . . .

CHESPER BEVER 1888-1925

MODERN WOODSMAN OF THE WORLD . . .

Jericho
unearthed 1952,

oldest community
still inhabited, sifting
through dust in the rock tell
for shards of the story, learning
as much from the garbage
as from great statuary . . .

Stone half buried in snow,
cockeyed, in the section
where they don't know who's buried for certain,
the pattern of the cross in the stone,
once perhaps colored marbles fit in these half-spheres,
this labor of love, monument to child or wife, who knows?
And the New Year struts in wearing her mask,
the old woman in the tattered dress,
dancing! dancing! ugly and shameless,
hair full of weeds, eyes as blind as
half spheres pressed in stone,
she midwifes us into suffering
one more orbit around the sun,
for some of us, the last one . . .

42.

GOD OF REAPING,
THE OLD GOAT,
RINGED
WITH ROCKLETS
IN HARMONIC DIVISION
NO MORE THAN 5 KM THICK
WHEN FIRST VIEWED BY GALILEO
HE THOUGHT THEY WERE EARS . . .

Sometimes I think of each day's dead
standing in long lines, naked, corpulent, ugly and sad
like prisoners herded toward the crematorium
while mad musicians fiddle and grin,
and Eichmann like Charon with a swaggerstick .

91

                                        POLYMORPHISM, EACH ATTRIBUTE
                                            DEIFIED SO THAT THE GODS
                                                DROP IN FOR DINNER
                                                    OR TO RAPE YOUR
                                                        DAUGHTER
                                                    (LONG-NECKED
                                                SWAN, THE GREAT PHALLUS)
                                            AND YOU NEVER WANT TO GET
                                        ONE OF THEM PISSED AT YOU, ASK
                                    ODYSSEUS WHO BLINDED THE WRONG POLY-
                                        PHEMUS, SUFFERED TEN YEARS OF
                                            PENANCE TO POSEIDON . . .
                SEPTUAGESIMA,
                    THE CONVERSION OF ST. PAUL,
                        CAPRICORN RULES WITH TAURUS OVERHEAD,
                    EARTH AT PERIHELION AND SIRIUS
                IN CANUS MAJOR. TIME FOR
            HIBERNATION, REPAIRING EQUIPMENT.
    MUHAMMED IS BORN, AND DIZZY DEAN . . .
                                            By the ash graves
                                                at Dachau, by
                                                    thousands
                                                shoveled together,
                                            and they grow flowers,
                                        red flowers, the Bible open
                                    to Psalm 22, "My God, My God,
                                why hast thou forsaken me? . . ."
                        THYMINE
    DIONYSIAN MYSTERIES,
        GOD TORN AND EATEN, SPRINKLING THE FIELDS
            SO VINE AND OLIVE COME FROM SOIL,
                AT ELEUSIS THE CELEBRANT
                    PASSES THROUGH CIRCLES
                DISROBING TO STAND NAKED AT CENTER
            BEING GOWNED WITH GODLINESS ON THE WAY OUT
    AND THE CHRISTIANS MAKE EASTER OUT OF IT . . .

92

                              TITAN, TETHYS, ENCELADUS,
                              RHEA, DIONE, JANUS &
                              THE ODDBALL PHOEBE
                              DANCE RINGS
                              AROUND
                              RINGS . . .

Where can we put them all?
Fifty thousand in this city alone, everyday one or two
    brought here, even in ice and snow blowing
        across the astroturf into the chiseled rectangle,
            and the millions in New York, Chicago, Cleveland,
                Tokyo, London, Mexico City, Cairo,
                    thousands every day processed through
                morgue & mortuary to fill up
            one landfill or another, to hang
        in charnal house, each needing a separate place,
    each a headstone for history . . .

                                          IVORY LIVINGSTON . . .

POOH DAY, MILNE & MOZART . . .

                              & THE ROMANS WORSHIPPED AT
                              EVERYBODY'S ALTAR, DII MAJORES,
                              LARES & PENATES, U-NAME-IT SACRED
                              GROVES & VESTAL VIRGINS, JUST SO
                              YOU PAID UR TAXES & KEPT THE
                              PAX ROMANA, BURNED AN
                              OBLIGATORY INCENSE
                              ANNUALLY TO
                              THE CURRENT CAESAR
                              YOU COULD SIT WITH THE
                              BEST OF THEM IN THE COLOSSEUM
                              DRINKING BEER & ROOTING FOR THE
                              HOME TEAM . . .

                    THYMINE
What I am beneath all masks
    dances here a moment . . .

                              93

43.

. . . IS A PUBLIC OFFENDER IN THAT HE DOES NOT
RECOGNIZE THE GODS THAT THE STATE
RECOGNIZES . . . AND HAS
CORRUPTED THE YOUTH," THUS
ANYTUS, 399 B.C. GOES FOR THE
DEATH PENALTY . . .

body sags like a melon left out
in the garden all winter,
blotched with mold,
crust-thin,
each organ
twitching & the
eyes in morning mirror
questioning existence . . .

CYTOSINE

PORTER FLINT, COSMOS VELTZ

& HOMER COMPOSED IT 1,000 YEARS
AFTER THE FACT, HOW MAGNIFICENT WAS
AGAMEMNON, ODYSSEUS, HELEN &
THAT DREAM OF ACHILLES TO
DESERVE SUCH POETRY . . .

This week some smart-ass kids have spraypainted
obscene words on the stones. Silver & black paint.
FUCK YOU. EAT SHIT. How many years
of wind and rain will it take?
Less than ten actually, the unheroic act
dies quickly & is gone . . .

PATELLA BY
LIGAMENT
STRINGS FEMUR
TO TIBIA PROTECTING
THE CRUCIAL HINGE . . .

PEISISTRATUS (556) DICTATOR
OF ATHENS, OUSTING SOLON--A TYRANT,
YET HE BUILT UP THE CITY & ENCOURAGED THE ARTS . . .

air filled with soot, lungs
with cigarette smoke, graffiti on
public buildings, violence
against trees, soil &
human souls . . .

SYNOVIAL FLUID LIKE RAW EGG WHITE
TO LUBRICATE AND CUSHION . . .

THREE UNKNOWN

PERSONS

"THE PELOPONESEUS & ATHENS WERE FULL OF YOUNG MEN
WHOSE INEXPERIENCE MADE THEM EAGER
TO TAKE UP ARMS." THUCYDIDES, CHARONEA 338
& PHILIP/ALEXANDER COMING IN LIKE NAPOLEON
TO FINISH THE JOB . . .

Five thousand
years & there will be
no factories, no scribbled
walls. The earth survives us.
Obscenity will not last the season . . .

CYTOSINE
AND BY WAY OF
APOLOGY, HE TOLD THEM HE WOULD
AS SOON DIE AS QUIT ASKING QUESTIONS, ALTHOUGH
"AS YOU WILL NOT EASILY FIND ANOTHER LIKE ME" (GADFLY, PAIN
IN THE GLUTEUS) "I WOULD ADVISE YOU TO SPARE ME."
BUT THE VOTE WENT OTHERWISE . . .

44.

The child senses but does not
believe in death. Here
the simple stone of
INFANT DAVIE,
APRIL 1928,
here, where the
violets first come out
in a few months . . .

95

Not so much instructing as inspiring
        the pupil, getting them to
                believe in themselves, that's
                        the essence of it . . .

                                DECIDUOUS TREES APPEAR,
                                BIRCH, ELM, OAK, MAPLE AS THE SEA
                                DIVIDES NORTH AMERICA AND
                                ROCKY MOUNTAINS RISE UP
                                OUT OF SEDIMENT . . .

                    ADENINE
                We remember only
            fragments, stories, faces
        hung like icons, parents looming monoliths
    as time throws its shadow between us,
so that at forty-two I come to believe in death
    without desiring it, not afraid of it completely,
        though when I feel it snuffling my throat like a wolf
            perhaps then I will wimper, my little house
                crushed in the claw, pieces of it
                    sifting through the blue depths,
                a common sediment falling out of existence,
            black battering ram rushing at great speed
        to spread me across the windshield of a particular instant,
    some cancer, thrombosis, embolism bursting, or the slow
agonizing digging after breath, gargling the vacuum, then
    the release, click of door and we are out of it
        into what? Darkness? The Light
            of God? Music & voices?
                Mother & Father,
                    Tell me what it is . . .

                                To encourage
                                    another
                                into becoming
                            completely empowered,
                        be it athlete or artist,
                    is an almost religious act . . .

DINOSAURS EXTINCT,
WARM-BLOODED CREATURES DOMINATE,
SURVIVING COLD NIGHTS CARNIVOROUSLY . . .

                                All humanity buried here if you think
                                about it: the wrought iron fence
                                of J.S. Bach, Melville's
                                humped, white stone
                                and Emily's thin
                                obelisk,
                                Pound's monumental
                                bust in a wide green
                                space under the mountains
                                and Walter's mausoleum back by
                                the spruces, Marc Chagall beside the
                                lilac bushes, everyone worth
                                remembering is here in
                                imagination including
                                SAVANNAH WHITLEY
                                1854-1926
                                we are one in
                                the spirit . . .

ADENINE

Remember Harlan Kinney
who never cursed his boys yet demanded
almost without speaking it their complete
allegiance/dedication to excellence, James
Miller also, brighteyed, tenacious
whose teams took district
or did not, being winners
in either case for his
unswerving respect for the individual . . .

                                CRETACEOUS, 72 MILLION
                                (CAN YOU IMAGINE IT?) YEARS LOCKED
                                IN THE CANYON WALL AND STILL NO SIGN
                                OF THE ARROGANT APE . . .

It snows lightly today.

In Virginia, my mother's sister babysits
her grandson. My brother in Ohio with his pregnant wife
    and other brother just becoming a man, my sister
        with her pearl of sorrow, grandmother in Munich
            sharing the small apartment with the dog,
                all of them close to me as I walk,
                    singing under my breath,
                talking to them, though I can know
            nothing of their lives moment to moment beyond
        imagining them, icons, mythology making
    contact through sleepwaves of the soul,
or a tree rooting through time/space
    for nourishment from other lives so there be
        nothing left unsaid or unexplored . . .

                              And the entire town joined in
                                 the snakedance two miles
                                 out to his house to
                                    convince Bill
                                       Moffitt to stay just
                                 one more year with the
                              High School Band. Greater
                        love hath no man earned than this,
                              tears in their eyes as they
                                 begged him . . .

                              45.

    What if we should die here? she asks.
        The kids on their bicycles in mid-February
            threading the snowless paths as we walk.
        She misses her people and the Ohio country . . .
                              THYMINE
                                 Great cave
                                 at Lascaux, Cro-
                              Magnon meaning BIG,
                        Upper Perigordian, 23K b.c.

                              98

                              the shaman in deerskin dances
                      stabbing the mountain lion image &
                      they drove 100,000 horses off
                          the cliffs at Soltre,
                            1,000 wolly mammoths
                              at Predmost,
                                  Great Hall
                                of the Bisons
                            closed to visitors
                        unsacred, noisy, unclean
                      eroding, leeching the artwork
                  sacred only in ritual torchlight . . .

        Observation, notation,
        comparing this with that,
     describing without injecting commentary,
 the THING ITSELF in its purity captured,
     patterns in the sky, moon phases, repetitions,
         naming, classifying, differentiating,
             subclassifying, predicting
                 the pattern . . .

                              ELIZABETH & ALBERT POPPLETON
                              If it comes to that, I'll
                                never leave, I say.
                                  If it comes to
                                      that, you'll
                                  do as you please.
                              (Where will we lie?
                          Who can imagine it?) . . .

                 Smeared red ochre
            on the corpse prior to burial.
         Survived the glacial ages, invented
      the needle, boots, caps & coats, leggings against snow,
  following the migratory reindeer, caribou, crossing over
Bering landbridge and possibly ocean as well, Clovis people,
    20K to 10K in Taima-Taima, Pikimachay, Monte Verde,
        Boqueirao da Pedra Furada & Backwater Draw . . .

Experimenting to prove hypothesis,
imagination submissive to data,
weighing and measuring,
mathematics the common
denominator . . .

THYMINE
What bird is that? A single
high-pitched note.
He's calling to his mate.
Once more, shrill. Where
are the children now?

Venus of
Brassempouy, ivory
coiffed goddess & the
black baked clay Venus of
Dolni Vestonice, 25,000 years
this ancient wonderment of
breasts and loveliness
and our doorway
into life,
split between
her thighs . . .

We'll live a long time, you'll see.
My arm around her, the trees arching over us,
and night coming on like a blanket of darkness,
colors sinking into the dry leaves, treelimbs,
deep blue water running into the sky
and translucent rind of new moon over the hills.
Who can explain this life?
There is no advancement in culture,
only tiny centers of peace against confusion,
where strength is stored for a time, then pulled apart
into myriad, disparate elements whirled away
over a field of grass & stones.
I have crossed a watershed ridgeline in my life.
We lean against each other as we walk . . .

46.

                              Alamogordo 7-16-45. Wedges
                                of U235 achieve critical
                                  mass & 2 septillion
                                    atoms fizz at
                                      once . . .

            Oldest fossils 3.1 billion b.c.
            bluegreen algae, cryptozoaic,
        printed like a negative . . .

                                      Winter silence
                                  commanding the still,
                                empty husk, face thin &
                              hollowcheeked, relaxed, the
                          muscles letting go, lips in a slight
                                smile. Christ, I never want it
                                  but what can you do? . . .

          CYTOSINE
      Weight based on carbon, 12
    atomic mass units capable of transformation
        through bombardment, alpha particles reduce
            weight by two amu's. Neils Bohr visualized
                shells & quantum leaps, 1913 . . .

                                  Classic: fly in amber.
                                      99.9999999999%
                                          disappeared
                                      w/o a trace.
                                  What we find stands
                                for the whole family . . .

            The apple tree
                in the vacant lot across the alley,
              branches black against snowblue twilight sky.
          I think of my father's overbearing presence,
            turned mellow and harmless in the muted dark.
        On the ground, a few frostbitten apples
      clutched in snow-filled furrows of the abandoned garden.
          Let me stand between you and the chainsaw . . .

101

TONY FABRIZIO, 1853 - 1934 . . .

minerals penetrating cellwall to
petrify, glorify, bronze poured
into the clay core . . .

"Little Boy," plugged like Frankenstein, Meitner & Frisch '38
& later Fermi w/Albert's
blessing burst in
1/1,000,000
second
8-6-45 92,000
dead or missing . . .

Nothing that has lived
is lost, but that it come again
revealed in others, your face in my face,
your song and vigorous walk in my swinging stride &
singing voice. The grass knows this even in winter.
Trees proclaim it, though they are sawed to pieces,
branches littering graves, fragrence
of cut timber on the air,
frozen footsteps cupping
rinds of snow . . .

CYTOSINE

It's all there to be
discovered, Mary
Leakey poking
the strata, finger-
prints filed in under-
ground vaults, chalk cliffs,
tar pits, ooze solidified around
wolly mammoth, hard evidence . . .

Dürer's
Horseman, skeletal,
clappering over the dry hedge
on his gaunt steed, the stiff-faced thing
in the box once was liquid & vibrant for a bit of time,

102

a ragged, painful patch of infinite days, stark skullbone
scythe & hourglass swinging, the undertaker close
behind, wiping his tools on a cloth. ee:
"reaped their sowing and went their came
sun moon stars rain" . . .

47.

QUINQUAGESIMA.
SEXAGESIMA. SHROVE
TUESDAY, ASH WEDNESDAY, GROUND
HOG DAY, BUDDY HOLLY KILLED 1959 & LINCOLN
TENNESSEE WILLIAMS JACK BENNY GRANT WOOD
WILLIAM TECHUMSEH SHERMAN & OLD GEORGE ALL
BORN. MARS IN THE HEAD
OF SCORPIUS . . .

MUEZZIN CALLING FROM MINARET:
THERE IS NO GOD BUT ALLAH
AND MOHAMMED IS HIS
PROPHET THREE
TIMES OVER FIVE TIMES
EACH DAY FACING MECCA THE
FAITHFUL REMEMBER THIS . . .

I am hungry for warmth,
for supple grass and leaves
and perfume of violets at evening,
the featherless birdling blown
from the high notch, blue
on the iced asphalt . . .

SHARKS 80 FEET LONG, SABRE TOOTHED
CATS, HORSES, WOOLY RHINO &
CAVE BEAR & THE GREAT APE
SHAMBLING ALONG . . .

GUANINE
GOD THE CREATOR IS JUST AND MERCIFUL.
EYE FOR AN EYE, HAND FOR THE THIEF,
ADULTERER BEHEADED, THE WOMEN VEILED

103

EXCEPT IN PARADISE WHERE HOURIS ATTEND
THE SLAIN WARRIOR VERY SENSIBLE CONCEPT
OF AFTERLIFE IF YOU ASK ME,
ESPECIALLY TO MOTIVATE JANISSARIES
FOR THE JIHAD AGAINST THE INFIDEL,
ISRAEL OR THE GREAT SATAN . . .

Which wind will
blow me
out of the high
nest? Which hour of
which day of which year?
After five minutes it will all be
forgotten, my stilled blood
absorbed by the spongy
darkness . . .

ROLLS LIKE A BIG, GREEN
BICYCLE ON ITS TINY RING, SIDEWAYS,
ATTENDED BY ARIEL, UMBRIEL, OBERON,
MIRANDA, TITANIA . . .

DISLIKED
BELLS & IMAGES
OF MEN OR BEASTS . . .

DR. TSUNEKICHI KIHARA, 1945 . . .

GUANINE
SEASON OF WATERS, THE DEAD
RISING OUT OF THE MUD TO SING
LIKE FROGS, THE STONE
ROLLED AWAY BY WINDS,
MERCURY LOW IN THE
WESTERN SKY,
WET PATHWAYS &
CRINKLED SEEDS . . .

QU'RAN (RECITATION)
ONE WHO SUBMITS TO ALLAH
IN THE PLACE OF KNEELING,
ENDING RAMADAM WITH THE LITTLE BAIRAM,
AND THE GREAT HAJJ TO MECCA ONCE IN A LIFETIME.

ABSTAIN FROM ALCOHOL. GIVE ALMS FREELY.
GUARD THE WIDOW AND ORPHAN. LIVE SIMPLY IF THAT IS POSSIBLE
WITH MORE THAN ONE WIFE. INSHALLAH.
ALLAH AKBAR . . .

48.

EVEN THE INTERSTICES FILLED WITH
DUST, WANDERING HYDROGEN ATOMS, NEBULAE
& COMETS, THE OORT CLOUD ASWARM
WITH OVER 100 BILLION OF 'EM
LONGHAIRED HALLEY, ENCKE
IKEYA-SEKI AND
KOHOUTEK . . .

AT SUSA A MIXTURE, SEMITES
& ARYANS, UR, ERIDU, URUK & BY
4,500 B.C. THEY HAD THE POTTER'S WHEEL,
COPPER WEAPONS & WEDGEPOINT WRITING,
TONS OF CLAY TABLETS, HISTORIES OF THE KINGS . . .

Connectedness.
Melody by Debussy, La
Mer, late winter snow curled
around treebase, overhead the
outreaching bud-studded branches . . .

ADENINE
BALLS OF ICE, SWUNG ON THE LONG CORD
TO WHIP PAST THE SUN SHOWERING CRYSTALS INTO THE WIND
ONCE IN A GENERATION . . .

tibia & fibula driving the
structure downfield,
kicking & climbing,
running fer yer
life . . .

dreamy floating awareness of time's roundness,
the great, lyrical latticework behind which the white-blue
bottomless ocean of air surges with clouds,
all visible stars in the basket along with

105

                    the entire human family over ten million years,
                 separate souls yearning for each other
              despite achievement unfulfilled w/o this touching,
           so that our grief is natural and dignified,
     important to perform as we honor each other,
           the roots spreading everywhere,
                 through the soil, through the air,
                    fibrous filaments . . .

                                                  ADENINE
                                        LOUIS G. MONTOYA . . .

                 solus extenser, digitorum
                    longus, tibialis anterior,
                 peroneus longus, extensor retinaculum,
              tendo calcaneus (achilles) . . .
                                        MURRAY GELL-MANN 1969
                                     FOR QUARK THEORY, CARLO RUBBIA
                                  OF CERN FINDING THE WEAK FORCE W+
                                     W- Z NAUGHT, 1984 N.P. . . .

              HATSHEPSUT BEARDED & BREASTLESS
           RULED TILL 1479, HER MAGNIFICENT COLLONADE OUTSIDE THEBES
     AND AFTERWARD, THUTMOSE III, HER BROTHER, ROUTED SYRIANS AT HAR-MEGIDDO
           ESTABLISHING EMPIRE, STRONG NAVY, TRIBUTE FROM ETHIOPIA
              AND THE COPPER MINES OF PERSIA, ALLTHINGS COME
                 FROM EGYPT CIRCE 3,500 B.C. THROUGH XXVI
                    DYNASTIES UNTIL ALEXANDER,
                       EVEN MONOTHEISM, IKHNATON
                    ESTABLISHING AKHETATON, CITY
                 OF THE SUN, BUT THE PRIESTS OVERCAME HIM
              & THE PEOPLE PREFER THEIR TRADITIONS, INVENTORS OF
           CLOCK, GLASS, CALENDAR, PAPER & INK,
     LINEN, PYRAMID, LIST GOES ON & ON . . .

                                        the grass pushing through
                                           crust of icy snow,
                                              keep a thin
                                                 greeness
                                              within you . . .

                                106

HORSEHEAD NEBULA,   CRAB SUPERNOVA
        WITH PULSAR AT ITS CENTER
            RECORDED BY SKYWATCHERS 1054 A.D.
                THE SEVEN SISTERS, RING IN LYRA
                    & TRIFID, BIRTHPLACE OF STARS . . .

                                I AM NEBUCHADREZZAR
                                    KING OF KINGS, STAMPED ON
                                EVERY BRICK IN BABYLON, DIORITE
                            CYLINDER OF HAMMURABI UNEARTHED AT SUSA,
                                ZIGGURAT 650 FEET TALL TOWER OF
                                    BABEL MEANS GATE OF GOD . . .

                "every atom belonging to me
            as good belongs to you" (literally) and
        I am so damned delighted by it all
    in that wine-loosened flowering of sensation,
a living bean, open to sound & light, heroism of the species
        surviving in spite of suffering--patience! patience!
            time like heavy water blue in the air,
                soft light seeping out of the ground like mist,
                    contains all ancestors chemically
                        bound in each bloodcell,
                    celebrating body parts,
                touching all private places without embarrassment,
            belonging, connected to it all,
        wet spots on stone benches,
dry tendrils clutching the fence wire,
        dish-white moon behind long strands of the branches . . .

                            49.

                                MALANSANGERR.
                                    GAGUDJU PEOPLE.
                                        GONDWANALAND.
                                    ULURU/AYERS ROCK . .

        PLEISTOCENE, HOLOCENE,
            MAKING THE SCENE WITH THESE TEMPORARY
                HUMAN BEINGS . . .

                            107

                                        For each, an opposite.
                                  Mutual attraction/annihilation
                                leaving a few cosmic rays . . .

                   delicate ice stars
                across mud puddles,
            time of preparations,
         table set with linen,
      dancers hired . . .

                                  the mirror self travelling an opposite
                                  life destined to meet me headon
                                       at our mutual explosion
                                            into one energy . . .

THYMINE
      CANYON DE CHELLY,
         THE ANASAZI SAFE IN THE BELLY,
            MUDSWALLOWS, CUT STONE, ECHOES
               FROM THE GREAT KIVA . . .

                                            Sharp white stone.
                                                 Infinite blue.
                                            God in the air.
                                       Permanence of allthings.
                                  White marble roof of the
                                  mausoleum against cobalt heaven.
                               Incarnation of Holiness, God's face
                                  swimming through my tears . . .

                     UNNATURAL.
                  DEFORESTATION, STRIP
               MINING, FLUOROCARBONS LEACHING OZONE,
            GREENHOUSE EFFECT, CLEARCUTTING, DDT,
         EXTINCTION OF SPECIES, POISONING
      OCEANS, SMOG, SEWAGE, CITIES, CIVILIZED MAN . . .

                                  EASTER ISLAND, TIERRA
                                       DEL FUEGO, PATAGONIANS,
                                            EATING THE GOD . . .

      & we walk here, my daughter & I, like
         mummers in costume, stomping & stamping,
            breaking the puddleice, dry wastage of old grass,

blown paper, dark ages, reading names
out loud in dramatic voices . . .

MARY ESTELLE

SHOEMAKER, 1925-1932 . . .

gamma rays hitting the
atmosphere create
electron/positron showers . . .

I am ready for spring,
but not all at once. One
blade at a time, birdsong audible,
intrusive, sparkling, custodians
raking the leaves away . . .

FRIED GENITALS GROUND INTO POWDER,
SPRINKLED ON THE LAND . . .

BREAKDOWN OF FAMILIES,
OF FOODCHAINS . . .

Come easy on me.
Slow, with majesty.
I cannot bear to have you
all at once . . .

50.

GUANINE

Take off our masks,
morning after Mardis Gras,
streets strewn with confetti,
rainswirled, naked & humorous,
trees resurrected with the tulips . . .

How we live
and work together,
psychology, demography, community,
case studies in relationships, fashion, trends,
caste/class, culture conflicts, revolutions, slavery, war . . .

7 tarsals, 5 metatarsals,
14 phalanges . . .

& death only a form of exile, a journey
    in which we are remembered by those we abandon
        (homebound held dear as well by voyagers outbound),
            so we are together, though blown apart like seeds,
                underfoot, connected in heart's soil,
                    a new stone for David
                    after forty-six years . . .

this communal dancing
choreographed by
hormones,
circling each other
arms out, hands almost
touching, then pulled away,
the courtship strut, ceremonial
heelturn hands-in-pockets scuff away
of the outcast, improvised soft-
shoe suicidal performances
for no audience, how
to understand
all this
irrational
damned behavior . . .

        dactylic, iambic, trochaic
        not to mention variable feet
    all running in irregular lines
held together by long plantar ligament . . .

                why should we give the
                hereafter a minute's thought?
            It is all as perfectly prepared
            as this world was when we
                entered kicking & screaming
                into good hands . . .

                    calcaneus,
                    talus,
                    navicular,
                    transverse arch . . .

                    the bride approaches
                        in her veil of snowflowers,
                            breath scented with violets . . .
                                            & the sole supporter,
                                        thick pad of fatty tissue
                                    like cushion of air, connecting
                                        to the ground of all being
                                            & nothingness . . .
                    Relationships
                are all that matter finally.
            Here the great social writings & scriptures agree.
        Without each other we are emptyhearted and dissatisfied.
    Connected we have purpose, importance, reason to live and die.
GUANINE *Belonging is our immortality . . .*
                                        Winter was only
                                            fooling after
                                                all . . .

                    51.

            Let it begin with dance,
                ceremonial buck-n-wing twostep turkeytrot
                    and the god enters naked
                like Baryshnikov airborne
            through 50,000 years,
        Isadora in gauze with her arms lifted,
    the trees with their arms lifted, windfilled, drunk with it,
music or no music, hands and feet in motion patterning space,
    kicking and leaping, drunk with it . . .
                                        "white man got
                                    no dreaming." Before
                                counting of sunrise when
                            silence filled spaces between stars
                        each man in his tribe, his story
                            danced & sung to children in the
                                long peace, the Dreamtime
                                    before brick & wall

                    111

                                        wheel & war . . .
                                              CYTOSINE
On my wall one of those nice
        National Geographic maps of the
            Universe showing our exact position . . .
                                        IN THIS MONTH
                                        MASSASOIT AND THE
                                        PILGRIMS FORMED THE
                                        LEAGUE OF FRIENDSHIP . . .
            THERESA LEONARDA MAZZARINI, 1932 . . .
                              sarabande, allemande, pavan . . .
        EQUINOX ON THE 20th,
    HALLEY'S COMET VISIBLE THIS YEAR,
THE MESSIAH FIRST PERFORMED, IN IRELAND
WITH A MALE CHORUS, TIME FLIES OVER US
BUT LEAVES ITS SHADOW BEHIND . . .
                              break it apart now, the sky
                                    a tatter of broken limbs,
                                        residue of winter not
                                            offensive, snow
                                                hail & the
                                            muddy boards the
                                        coffin rests on . . .
        bushmen still live that way
            despite airplanes carving the sky
                our noise & refuse pushing their backs
                    against the timewarp . . .
                                    MANURE THE GROUND.
                                    GET OUT YOUR DANCING SHOES.
                                    SKUNKS ARE MATING . . .
            mysteries have been
        revealed to me . . .
                              Matisse pictures them sitting
                                    simply on the ground (red)
                                        playing flute and
                                            singing . . .
        Kabuki . . .
                                    112

                                        All time

                                    centers in this

                                place. One stone

                            stands for every face . . .

NEPTUNE RULES: SIGN OF THE FISH . . .

CYTOSINE

                                They are burying those who

                            cannot face another April . . .

GODS IN THE SKY AT NIGHT,
    BOBBIE FROST BORN 1874 & JACK BENNY'S
        RADIO DEBUT, PEEPERS HEARD IN DEDHAM, MASS 1748
            AND JOHANN SEBASTIAN BACH 1685, HARRY
                HOUDINI 1874 ESCAPED THE WOMB
            AS JESUS ESCAPED THE TOMB THIS SUNDAY,
        ANTARES OCCULTED BY THE MOON, THIS IS
    VISIBLE ONLY IN THE PACIFIC NORTHWEST . . .

                            slowly, with great dignity,

                                entering from the edges,

                                    each step governed

                                        and lyrical . . .

I am thinking of the 6th Symphony, "Pastorale,"
light spreading around me on the loosening grass,
    grandeur of vanished kingdoms, twelfth century tapestries,
        exotic birds, white berries like puckered skulls,
            melody played on an ivory flute,
                the graves of two lovers, limestone and roses . . .

                            burning the rainforests for farmland,

                                ancient mother of all humanity,

                                    red soil running into the

                                        Amazon like blood . . .

                oh how they bend to it,

            and there is no end to it,

        twisting untwisting hands interlinked

    then unlinking as the

entire ensemble comes apart like

unzipping a zipper, the long sinuous crystalline

    strands curling out into darkness looking for partners . . .

113

52.

There is a quiet time at the end of things,
        winter's aftermath, the paper-mache mask of a wasp's nest
            blown across isolated patches of snow,
                footprints in mud, the first birds jabbering

                                        QUETZALCOATL

A BLACK HOLE HAS NO HAIR

                            mornings of smoky breath,
                                evenings of clear, cool sunlight

        A BAA'THINA'HU
        A BAA'THINA'HU
                    THE CEDAR TREE
                    THE CEDAR TREE

                                    ghosts that sleep in
                                        pale roots, the first
                                            white crocus

            CHANDRASEKHAR LIMIT

CLEVELAND HORTON, ELUTERIO DEHERERA, LINDA BEGAY

        I PRAY WITH THE PIPE IN THE FOUR DIRECTIONS
        GREAT SPIRIT, BLESS OUR MOTHER EARTH

                                    GENIUS IN WHEELCHAIR,
                                FLESHBOUND BUT UNBOUNDED,
                            WHO WITH R. PENROSE DEFINED
                        SINGULARITY, 1970

        homecoming of sorts, although
        I cannot say if I am returning
    or if earth is prodigal

                        114

WAKANTANKA

                                        HAVE PITY ON ME.
            I WANT TO LIVE, THEREFORE I DO THIS

        turning in circles in the wide grassy field at the end
    of the cemetery, the road leading into the untended weeds, sagebrush and the
        naked hillside with its tumbled rocks, each detail remembered
            from ages past, yet disconcertingly fresh, unfamiliar, this
                time at the beginning of things when all that
                    has been and is to be hang together in pensive balance,
                        earth motionless day to day, an ecstasy
                            of anticipation

                                        FRIENDS OF WAKINYAN
    I PASS THE PIPE TO YOU FIRST,
        CIRCLING I COMPLETE THE FOUR QUARTERS AND THE TIME.
            I PASS THE PIPE TO THE FATHER WITH THE SKY.
                I SMOKE WITH THE GREAT SPIRIT.

                                REDUCTIO AD ADSURDUM:
                                THERE MUST BE A REGION OF
                                SPACE-TIME FROM WHICH NOTHING
                            NOT EVEN LIGHT CAN ESCAPE

                    HA'TNITHI'AKU'TA'NA
                    HA'TNITHI'AKU'TA'NA
                            WE HAVE IT IN THE CENTER
                            WE HAVE IT IN THE CENTER

                                lie down on the soft swell
                                    at the center of space/time
                                        penetrating the universe

        YOU MUST NOT FIGHT, DO NO HARM TO ANYONE, DO RIGHT ALWAYS.
                THUS WOVOKA, MESSIAH
                            TO THIS END, MY CHILDREN,
                        MAY YOU BE BLESSED WITH LIGHT

                            115

April arrives on a warm wind in the night

                    MOTHER CORN, GRANDFATHER ROCK

          long string of memory unwinding like a rosary each bead a name a
                    face oh god have i lived this long to have such a
                         string of prayers blowing out behind me?

                                                                    CYTOSINE
                                        /
GUANINE

                    LAWRENCE CRABTREE, PABLO ZUNIGA, WILLIAM SELF

                                             trees resurrected amid violets
                                               ah, violets, first delicate
                                                  scent like a thin string

                    NEUTRON STARS PULSING THE POWER OF CREATION

          HOZHONI, HOZHONI, HOZHONI

and the survivors celebrating sunlight,
          winter's beard cut off and thrown away like a wasp's nest,
               buds unfolding like buddhas overhead--open the windows!
               let fresh air blow into the soul!

                                                            HOZHONI

          AT THE CENTER OF OUR GALAXY, THE MILKY WAY, IS A BLACK HOLE
               INTO WHICH STREAMS A CLOUD OF GAS 90 TRILLION MILES STRUNG OUT
               LIKE A PRAYER BEAD PULLING STARS TO THE CENTER

                         FIRST DAY, BUFFALO SKULL AND DANCE
                         SECOND DAY, HONOR THE GREAT BEAR
                         THIRD DAY, ERECTION OF SACRED POLE
                    FOURTH DAY, OFFERING BLOOD AND PRAYERS

                                        we know nothing, dream everything

        ONE TEASPOON = THE MASS OF ONE MILLION SUNS

                    HOZHONI, HOZHONI

                        THYMINE/ADENINE

                                            HOZHONI
        THE EARTH, ITS THOUGHTS ARE MY THOUGHTS

                                Hosannah

            HOZHONI

                        THE BIG CRUNCH

                sacred syllables

                                    dance together

                                            PULLING ALL POINTS
        INTO THE CENTER

                    behold:

                                a million dancing shadows

            follow you

                                        HOZHONI

                                117

unending

                              inbreathing

        INTO YOUR MIDST HAS COME A NEW LIFE!

exhaling

                                    om

                  eg

                                a

A BRIEF GUIDE TO THE PERPLEXED -- TWELVE STRANDS TWISTED TWELVE TIMES

THE MOUNT MORIAH STUDIES was originally written in 1975 as a lyrical
meditation in relatively straightforward poetic lines patterned after
Whitman's SONG OF MYSELF, with one section for each week of the year
beginning in April. Four subsequent drafts later, it achieved this
finished form which is structured in imitation of the DNA molecule
(hence the use of the four bases ATCG to bind each section together)
and contains twelve separate themes or strands (one for each month)
which twist about each other in structured combinations. Each strand
is represented by a different typeface, either upper or lower case.
A key to the twelve strands is given below:

Artisan lower case: fragments from the original poem.

ARTISAN UPPER CASE: Twelve world religions or belief systems

Letter Gothic lower case: The physics of sub-atomic particles.

LETTER GOTHIC UPPER CASE: The physics of the universe, cosmology.

Bookface Academic lower case: The twelve parts of the human
body related to the signs of the zodiac for each month.

BOOKFACE ACADEMIC UPPER CASE: The signs of the zodiac,
planets, elements, historical events from the almanac.

Prestige Elite lower case: History of man's evolution.

PRESTIGE ELITE UPPER CASE: History of earth's evolution--geological ages.

Script lower case: Major branches of scientific study & academic discipline.

SCRIPT UPPER CASE: Human history from the present to prehistory.

Courier Italic lower case: Human crafts & professions for each month
of the year as related to the zodiac.

COURIER ITALIC UPPER CASE: Names from gravestones.

ORATOR LOWER CASE: THE FOUR BASES THAT BIND DNA TOGETHER: ATCG

In the first three seasons of the year, the "molecule" is rotated.
In the final season, it is split in half, signifying ends and beginnings.
Sources for this study were basically everything I could get my hands on.